THE COMPASSIONATE BODHISATTVA

Sidestone Press

THE COMPASSIONATE BODHISATTVA

Unique Southeast Asian images of the Bodhisattva Avalokiteśvara

Sofia Sundström

Published by Sidestone Press, Leiden
www.sidestone.com

Lay-out & cover design: Sidestone Press
Photograph cover: Avalokiteśvara from Java © pigprox | stock.adobe.com

ISBN 978-90-8890-617-6 (softcover)
ISBN 978-90-8890-618-3 (hardcover)
ISBN 978-90-8890-619-0 (PDF e-book)

1

Contents

For my mother,
Solveig Sundström (1942-2016),
who taught me to never turn down an adventure.

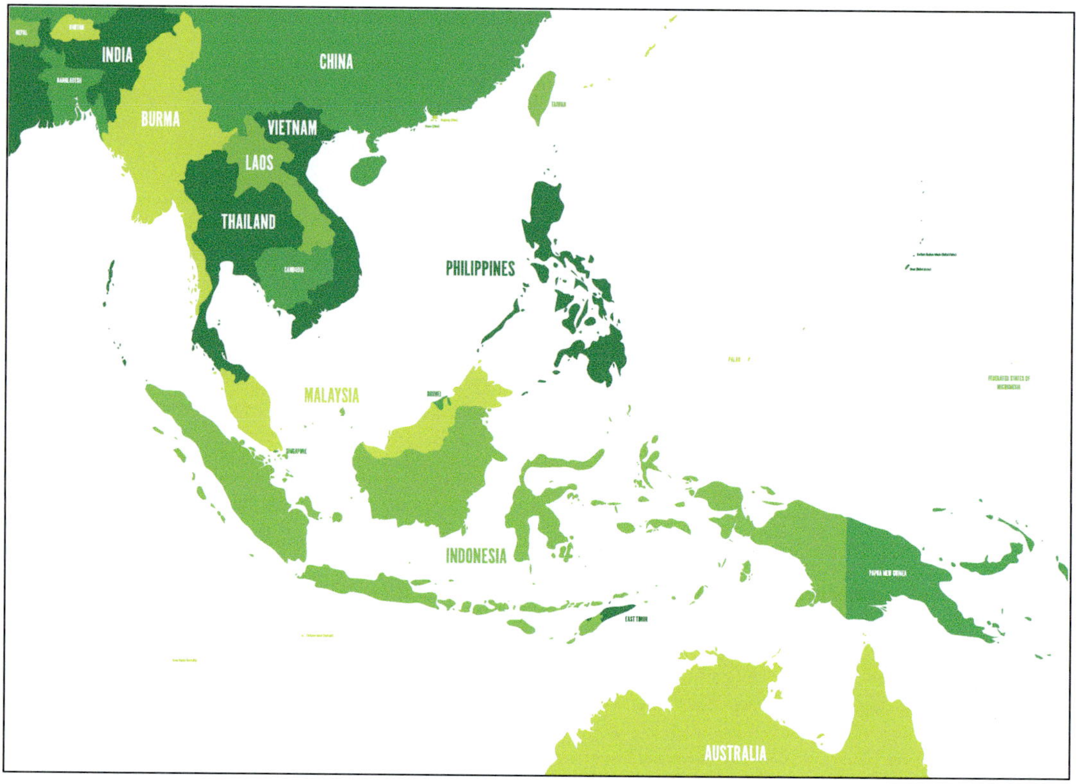

Image 1. Map of Southeast Asia.

1

Introduction

Southeast Asia has a long history with Buddhism that continues to the present day. More than 1,000 years ago, Buddhism spread to various areas of Southeast Asia through pilgrims, monks and merchants. It is in this region that some of the greatest Buddhist images and monuments were produced centuries ago. These include the majestic Borobudur in Central Java and the Bayon at Angkor Thom in Cambodia. Images of the Bodhisattva

What is a Bodhisattva?

As Buddhism developed over the centuries, the idea of Bodhisattvas evolved as a way to simplify the path to enlightenment. Once the Buddha reached nirvana after death (parinirvāṇa), where he became one with the universe, he could no longer be called upon for help and it is into this space that the Bodhisattva came into being.

The first Bodhisattva was actually the Buddha, or rather Siddhartha, before he reached enlightenment. His deeds as a Bodhisattva are described in the Jataka tales. A Bodhisattva functions as a teacher, but also generates Bodhicitta or compassion. There are many Bodhisattvas, but Avalokiteśvara and Maitreya are the most well-known. Avalokiteśvara represents compassion but is also the protector of the world. Maitreya is the future Buddha, but until then he is a Bodhisattva.

Avalokiteśvara were also produced in large numbers at this time and a few of these will be examined in this book.

Avalokiteśvara has been, and remains, the most popular Bodhisattva in the Buddhist pantheon. The Bodhisattva Avalokiteśvara is associated with compassion, which stems from his decision not to achieve enlightenment until all sentient beings have done so first. This is in part why Avalokiteśvara remains popular and current in modern society, we are still in need of compassion. Avalokiteśvara is also known as seeing and hearing the suffering of all sentient beings.

Compassion and Buddhist texts

In the eighth century CE, an Indian monk named Santideva wrote *The Compendium of Training (Śikshāsamuccaya)*, which explains in depth the conducts that Bodhisattvas must embrace. In the text, Santideva describes a Bodhisattva's infinite compassion:

> A Bodhisattva resolves: I take upon myself the burden of all suffering. I am resolved to do so, I will endure it. I do not turn or run away, do not tremble, am not terrified, nor afraid, do not turn back or despond (Conze *et al.* 2014: 131).

The Bodhisattva then continues to explain why he makes this choice of carrying the burden of suffering since it must be better that he alone should be in pain rather than have all

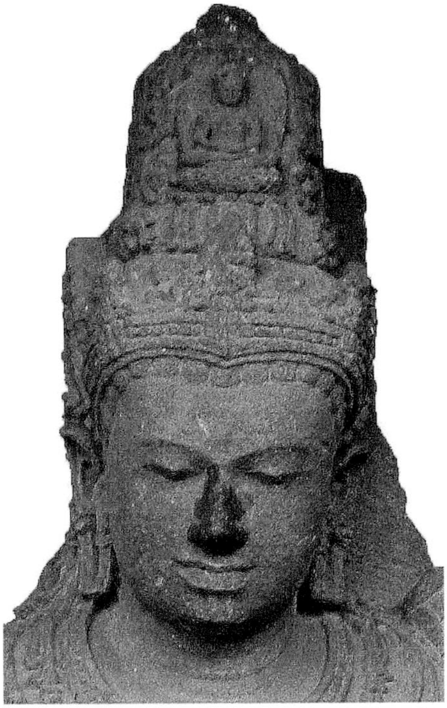

Image 2. Avalokiteśvara's headdress illustrating the presence of the Buddha Amitābha seated in mediation.

other beings suffer (Conze *et al.* 2014: 132). This is of course a logical choice, that it is better that one suffers rather than all, but who among us would be able to make such a choice? The Bodhisattva makes this choice as a part of his highest aim is to win all knowledge and wishes to set free all sentient beings.

The Bodhisattva Avalokiteśvara was born out of white light generated by his spiritual father, the Buddha Amitābha (Infinite Light). He is the Buddha of the West and resides in Sukhāvatī heaven or the Western Paradise. This is where a worshipper of the Buddha Amitābha can be reborn within a lotus. Avalokiteśvara, on the other hand, resides in this world, on Mount Potalaka, which is said to exist in southern India. In Avalokiteśvara imagery, his spiritual father is included in the headdress, where he sits in meditation (Image 2).

The name itself, Avalokiteśvara, means 'He who looks down on the world', thus, his capacity to witness all suffering is even included in his name. While Avalokiteśvara is filled with compassion, he also has great power. An early Buddhist text, the *Lotus Sutra* (*Saddharmapuṇḍarīkasūtra*) dated from 286 CE when it was translated into Chinese, describes him as being able to save merchants from shipwrecks or stop storms, an important quality in Southeast Asia as it was part of the Maritime Silk Route. Avalokiteśvara's powers do not stop with being able to calm storms, he can also break prisoners' chains and rescue a worshipper from robbers.

A slightly later Buddhist text, the *Kāraṇḍavyūhasūtra* (*Casket of the qualities of Avalokiteśvara*) dated to the end of the fourth century CE, deals exclusively with Avalokiteśvara and tells of how he travelled to hell. The text describes how the Buddha, Bodhisattvas, gods and goddesses were gathered together in the Jeta Grove, when they saw a fantastical white light emerge from another dimension, Avici hell. This light purified everything in the grove and the Buddha was asked from where the light was coming. He answered that the light was caused by Avalokiteśvara entering hell in order to save the suffering sentient beings. Despite Avici hell being surrounded by iron walls, they were unable to stop Avalokiteśvara who simply walked through them. He broke into hell, destroyed the torture implements and quenched the fires.

Once inside Avici hell, Avalokiteśvara entered the city of the hungry ghosts or pretas. These are beings who in life exhibited a strong animalistic urge and in death they have mouths the size of a needle's eye and can therefore never become satisfied. Standing inside the hell, rivers of water flowed from Avalokiteśvara's hands and feet, and when the hungry ghosts

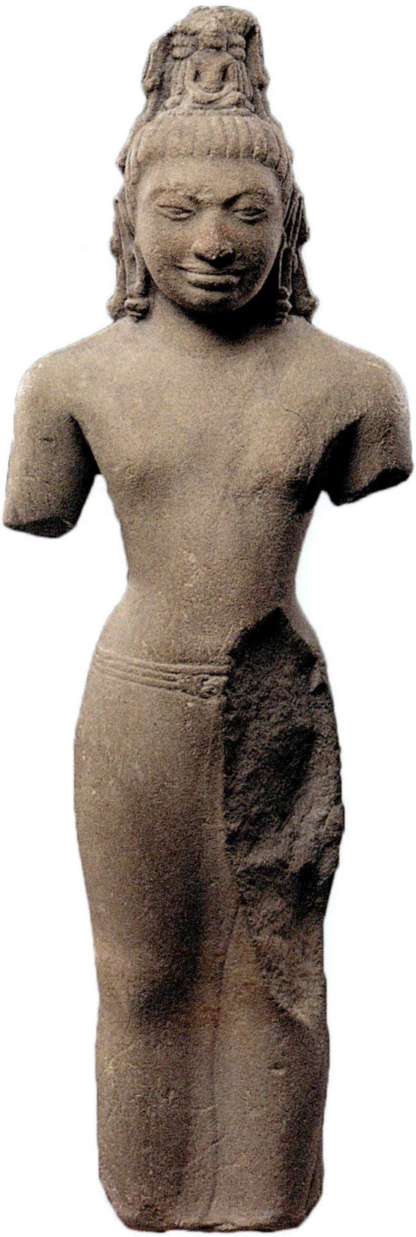

had drunk of this water their mouths and throats reached normal size and their bodies appeared healthy. Once he had saved these sentient beings, Avalokiteśvara continued to other worlds where others could be saved. This part of the *Kāraṇḍavyūhasūtra* illustrates Avalokiteśvara's compassion for all sentient beings.

Avalokiteśvara images in Southeast Asia

The Bodhisattva Avalokiteśvara remains a strong presence in today's Buddhist countries of Southeast Asia, such as Singapore, Thailand and Vietnam. However, 1,000 years ago he had a cultural impact across the region as we will see in this book. The earliest images of Avalokiteśvara in Southeast Asia show him in an ascetic form where he lacks any jewellery. The ascetic Avalokiteśvara image was inspired by several Buddhist texts that lauded the

Image 3. Ascetic Avalokiteśvara in the Metropolitan Museum of Art, New York. Acc. no. 1987.218.16.

ascetic ideal. The ascetic Avalokiteśvara images can first be seen at the Buddhist caves of Maharashtra in western India. There they are carved into the rock alongside a depiction of perils or dangers from which Avalokiteśvara can save his devotees.

The ascetic Avalokiteśvara is often depicted as standing and has two arms. These types of depictions have been found in various locations in the region, including Java, Sumatra, Thailand and Cambodia.

This example of the ascetic Avalokiteśvara can now be seen at the Metropolitan Museum of Art in New York (Image 3). It illustrates the style from southern Thailand in Peninsular Malaya and dates to the second half of the seventh century CE. It has a height of 45.1 cm and can easily be identified as Avalokiteśvara due to the presence of the Buddha Amitābha in his headdress.

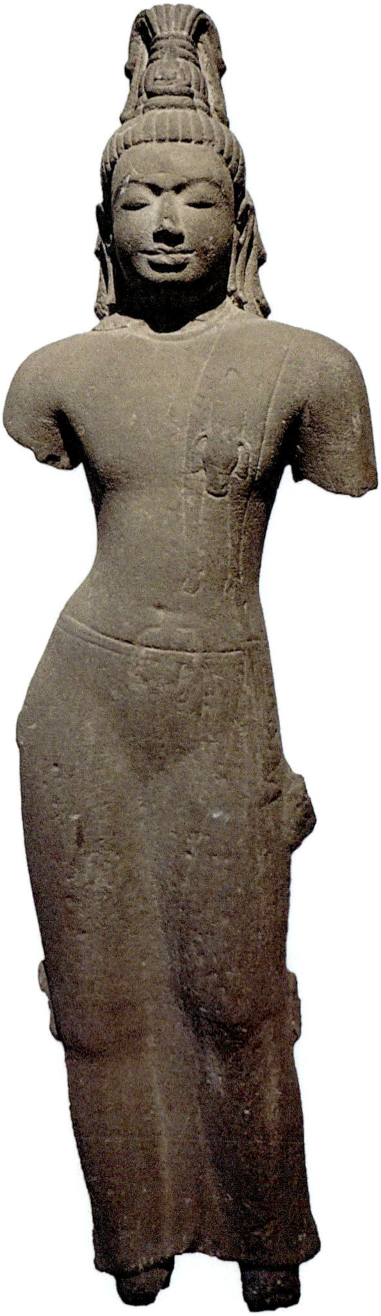

Image 4. Ascetic Avalokiteśvara stone statue with an antelope skin over the left shoulder in the Bangkok National Museum.

Both arms are now missing, but we can see that the Bodhisattva has a plain dress with a rope as a belt.

It is unknown how or exactly when the knowledge of this specific iconographic combination for Avalokiteśvara reached Southeast Asia. However, as the iconography was developed in Maharashtra it is possible that the knowledge travelled to Southeast Asia via ship, especially as there were many merchants in the area. The transfer of knowledge may also have occurred through travelling monks. We know of only a few monks who travelled from South Asia to China via Southeast Asia from their biographies, among these was the Chinese monk Yijing who will be discussed further in the chapter on Sumatra. However, the actual number of monks travelling to Southeast Asia would have been much higher.

A second example of the ascetic Avalokiteśvara was also found in southern Thailand in Chaiya, Surat Thani province (Image 4).

This tall stone statue, with a height of 1.14 m is on display at the National Museum in Bangkok. Unfortunately, both arms are now missing. Avalokiteśvara has a taller headdress in this image and the Buddha Amitābha is seated in meditation at the front. Avalokiteśvara does not have any jewellery, but wears an antelope skin over his left shoulder. The antelope skin is an attribute of the ascetic, a forest dweller, who clothes himself in animal skins and bark.

A fourth example of the ascetic Avalokiteśvara was found at Musi Ulu, near Palembang on Sumatra. It is now on display at the National Museum in Jakarta (Image 5).

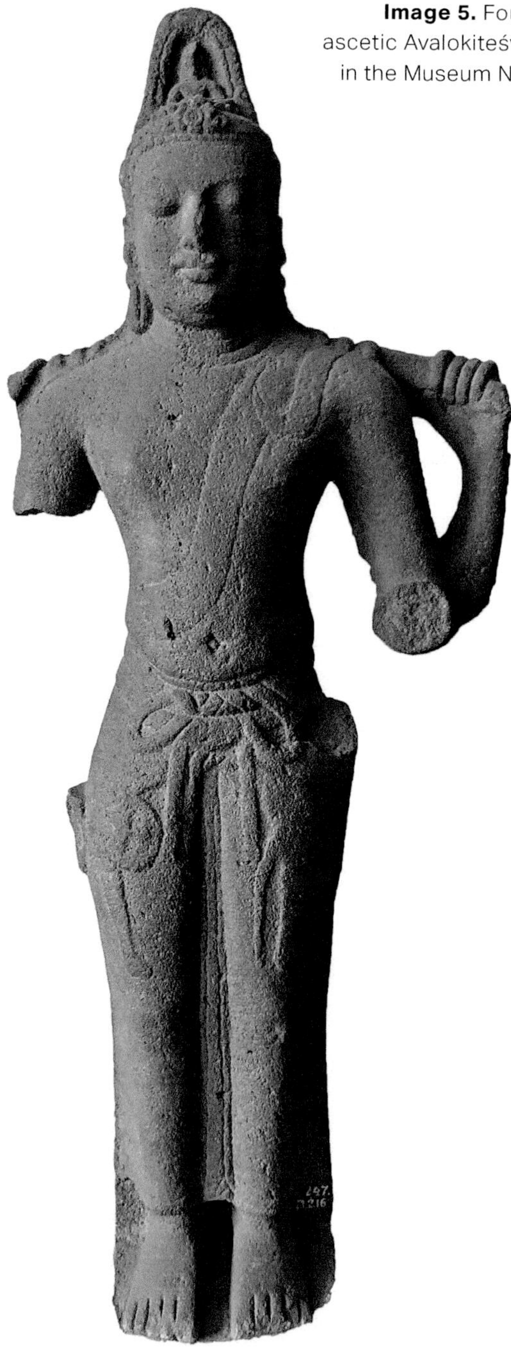

Image 5. Four-armed standing ascetic Avalokiteśvara from Sumatra in the Museum Nasional in Jakarta.

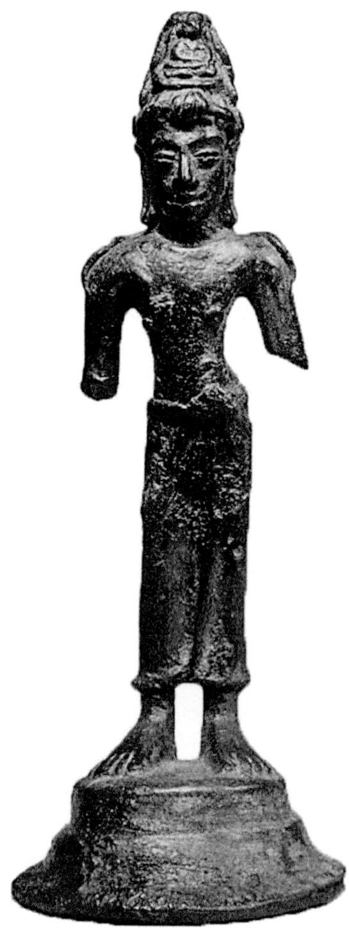

Image 6. Example of a two-armed ascetic Avalokiteśvara in bronze from Sumatra in the Metropolitan Museum of Art, New York. Acc. no. 1987.142.223.

This 1.72 m tall statue has the clear Buddha Amitābha in the headdress. Here, Avalokiteśvara is missing three of his arms, but the upper left hand remains intact and shows the Bodhisattva holding a palm-leaf manuscript. Avalokiteśvara does not have an antelope skin as in the previous stone statue, but wears a sacred thread in the form of a sash with a fold at the left shoulder. A sacred thread, or *yajñopavīta*, is often seen in depictions of Bodhisattvas and Hindu deities in Southeast Asia. Around the Bodhisattva's hips we see a tiger skin, an attribute for Avalokiteśvara which was developed in Southeast Asia or Sri Lanka.

We do not have textual references regarding the worshippers of Avalokiteśvara, but we do have images of the Bodhisattva from across Southeast Asia testifying that these worshippers did exist. We can also look at the size of the statues and deduce that they were likely used in a public setting, such as a temple, rather than in a more private ritual. Even though the knowledge of Avalokiteśvara came initially from South Asia, the local craftsmen, architects and monks developed their own methods for illustrating Avalokiteśvara as we shall see in the coming chapters.

Smaller statuettes have also been found of the ascetic Avalokiteśvara form on Java, Sumatra and Borneo, as well as in modern day Thailand and Cambodia (Image 6). These images date to approximately the seventh century CE, when the production of Buddhist and Hindu imagery had a similarity in both style and iconography across the region.

This similarity has been studied by different scholars, such as Pierre-Yves Manguin, and is referred to as a pan-cultural response to the influence of South Asia. His colleagues and him have identified several images that show a strong similarity and were found across Southeast Asia. One example is the many Vishnu stone statues found in the coastal areas of Vietnam, Thailand and Sumatra, quite a distance apart. One theory for this pan-cultural response is that the statues were produced in one location and then transported to different sites.

However, from eighth century onwards, the different regions of Southeast Asia began to develop their own style when illustrating the Bodhisattva Avalokiteśvara. In Vietnam, there was a strong stylistic influence from China, which led to Avalokiteśvara images with a style of dress unique to Vietnam in Southeast Asia.

2

Vietnam – a unique fashion style

Vietnam is one of the countries in Southeast Asia that has remained Buddhist. It borders China in the north and Laos, as well as Cambodia, in the west. Due to the geographical location of modern day Vietnam, Buddhism may have reached the area from South Asia or via China. Nevertheless, reach it it did. During the eighth to tenth centuries CE, the Vietnamese followed Mahayana Buddhism, which led to the production of Avalokiteśvara images. The area was then known as Champa. However, Shivaism was actually the more popular religion during the Champa period, but existed alongside Buddhism (Image 7).

Unfortunately, due to Vietnam's turbulent history, especially considering the Vietnam War, a great deal of the archaeological evidence of Champa has been destroyed. In some cases, we only have photographs of Cham buildings taken from the early 20th century.

There are, however, local and Chinese texts that paint a remarkable picture of sculptures made of gold and bronze. There must also have been wood sculptures and mural paintings, but none have survived. Nevertheless, even with our limited material evidence from the Champa period, we may still learn some things about this culture and their worship of the Bodhisattva Avalokiteśvara.

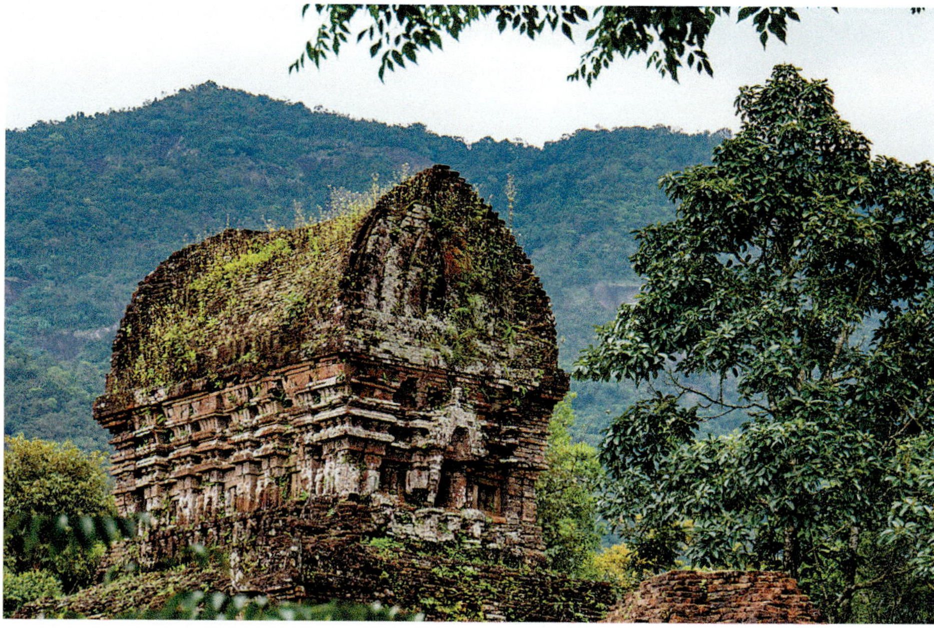

Image 7. Example of Champa architecture from the Hindu complex My Son.

The standing Champa Avalokiteśvara bronze statuettes have a specific mode of dress, epitomised by the stylised form of the belt sash as it drapes over the thighs. This sash is in addition to a belt with a decorated central clasp at the upper part of the garment. Two of these images will be examined in this chapter and they both have a similar style of lower garment. The centre of the garment has been pulled up, creating a herringbone pattern in the fabric. The pulled fabric is symbolised by a long flap that reaches the belt sash. Both of these bronze images show Avalokiteśvara with a tall headdress with the Buddha Amitābha at the front. The tops of the headdresses take the form of a lotus.

A bronze Avalokiteśvara is on display at the National Museum of Vietnamese History in Ho Chi Minh City (Image 8). It was found in 1960 in the district of Hoai Nhon in the Binh Dinh province. It has a height of 67 cm and is

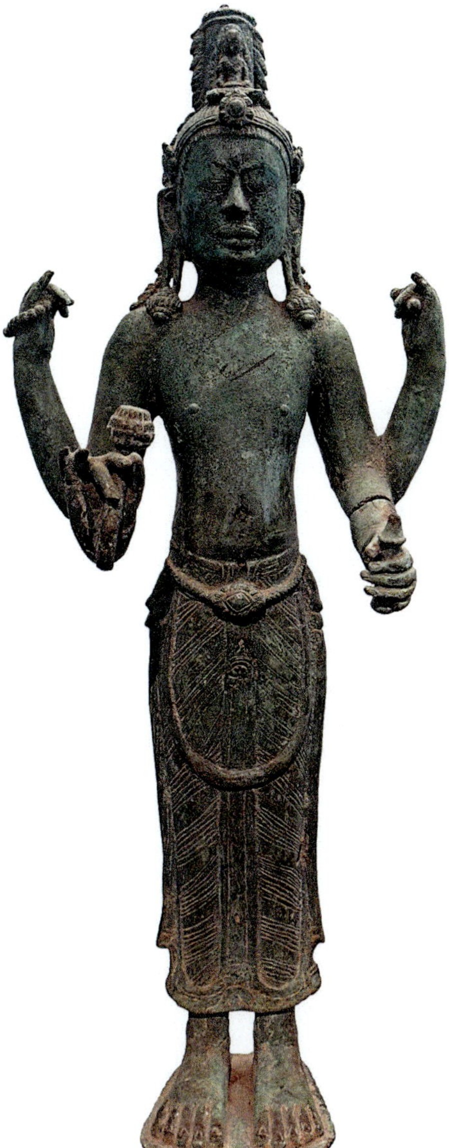

dated to approximately the eighth century CE. The bronze Bodhisattva wears bulbous earrings that rest on either shoulder. Behind the ears, we see strand of hair falling down and the headdress is decorated with a headband that has a floral central piece. In his upper right hand Avalokiteśvara carries a rosary and his lower right hand holds a lotus. In the upper left hand he has a book and the lower left hand holds a water vessel.

Here we see Avalokiteśvara with firmly closed eyes and full lips. He does not wear the sacred thread or a necklace, armbands or bracelets. Between the Bodhisattva's two eyes we see a third closed eye. The third eye is a rare attribute for Avalokiteśvara; it is more common for the Hindu god Shiva. Avalokiteśvara shares several attributes with Shiva, such as the tiger skin around his hips and the

Image 8. Four-armed ascetic Avalokiteśvara the National Museum of Vietnamese History in Ho Chi Minh City. Acc. no. BTLS 1290.

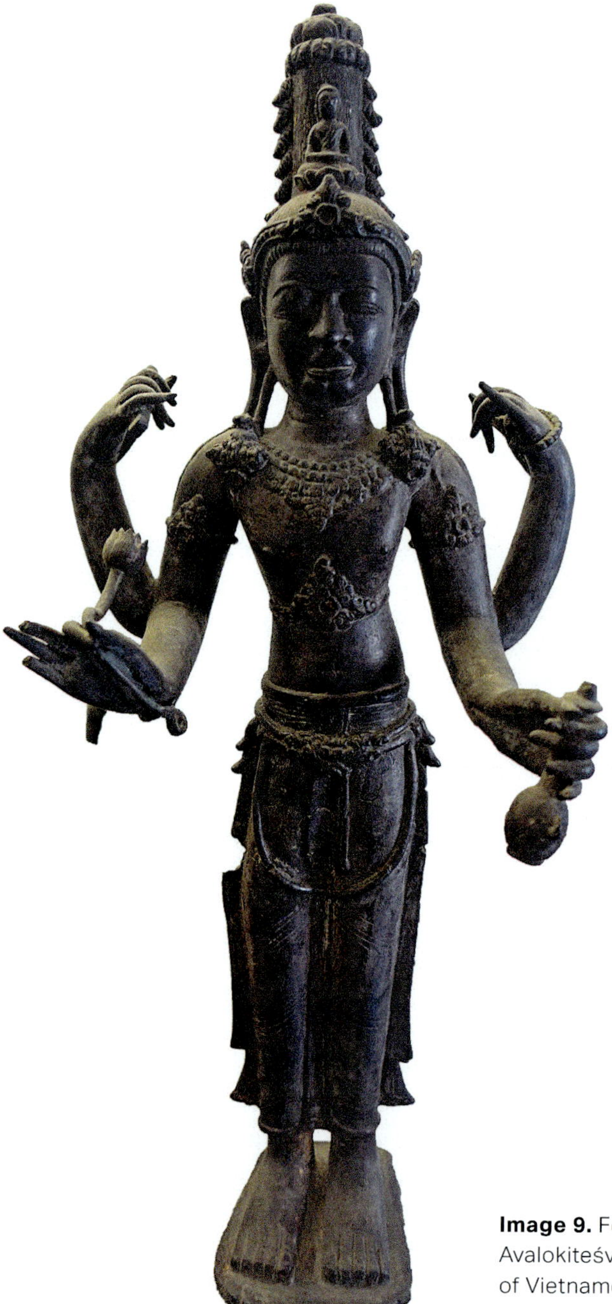

Image 9. Four-armed bejewelled Avalokiteśvara in the National Museum of Vietnamese History in Ho Chi Minh City. Acc. no. BTLS 1289.

antelope skin over his left shoulder. However, Shiva can be identified by a half-moon at the front of his headdress.

The second statuette also illustrates the same type of stylised dress, but has a slightly later production date. By then the local style had developed from the ascetic form to the princely form, where Avalokiteśvara wears more jewellery, such as a necklace and armbands. Avalokiteśvara still carries a water vessel, a feature of the wandering ascetic; thus, a few ascetic attributes remain.

The statue was found in a local temple near Dai Hui in Quang Binh province and is now on display at the National Museum of Vietnamese History in Ho Chi Minh City (Image 9). It is taller than the first image with its 75 cm.

Here, the Bodhisattva wears elaborate jewellery. He carries a broad necklace, armbands, bracelets, a chest belt and heavy earrings resting on each shoulder. It is this jewellery that gives us a later production date than the first statuette. He holds a manuscript in his top right hand and in the lower right hand a lotus. The upper left hand holds a rosary and the lower left hand carries a water vessel. The presence of the manuscript, as well as the rosary, links the image with the Buddhist texts that reference of Avalokiteśvara, such as the Lotus Sutra.

The lower garment has a slightly more exaggerated swallow's tail effect at the bottom than the first statuette's garment. Both statuettes have garments with incised lines creating a herringbone pattern. However, these bronze figures stand directly on a rectangular, flat piece. This type of attachment is not seen in other areas of Southeast Asia. Instead, the bronze statuettes may have been cast with tangs under the feet, which would be inserted into a base. Another possibility is that the figure and the seat would be cast together.

The size of these two bronze statues indicate that they would have had pride of place in a temple sanctuary. The soft manner in which Avalokiteśvara's face is depicted with his eyes closed in these two bronzes shows that he is in meditation, capable of listening to any prayers or concerns. He may in fact be listening with compassion. The idea of compassionate listening is part of the local Buddhism developed in Vietnam. Perhaps the most well-known representative of Vietnamese Buddhism in modern times is the monk Thich Nhat Hanh, who has spoken of compassionate or deep listening as a productive way to help relieve the suffering of another human being. It is essential that the person is allowed to express any thoughts without censure. If they exhibit what is called 'wrongful perception' you may address it at a later time, not during compassionate listening. By allowing the person to empty their heart you can help alleviate their suffering. In his meditative form, Avalokiteśvara may represent this quality of compassionate listening.

Scholars of Southeast Asian Buddhist art, such as Jean Boisselier, have indicated that these statuettes actually originated from Java. However, as we saw in the previous chapter, there was a centuries long period in Southeast Asia where there had been a pan-cultural response to outside artistic and religious influence. Thus, when each region began to develop their own artistic language, they all started with the same iconographic and stylistic information.

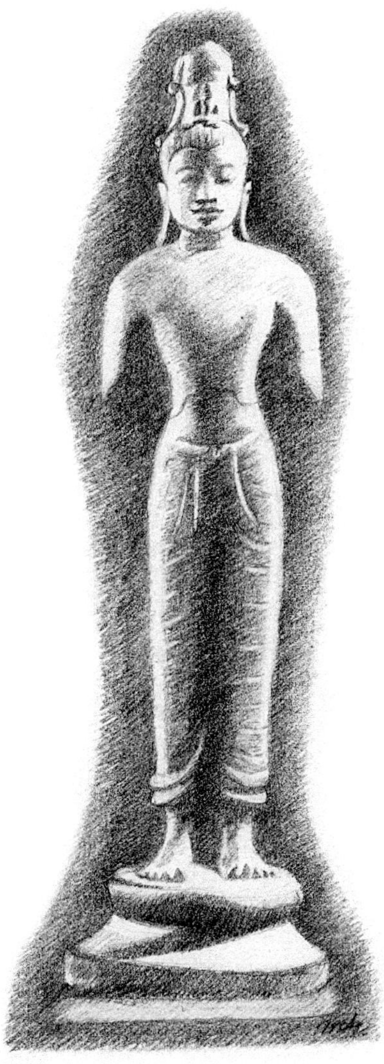

In terms of the Bodhisattva Avalokiteśvara, this knowledge would have included him standing and with two or four arms. These images would have little or no jewellery and a few may have had the antelope skin over one shoulder. In Champa, we see the local artistic language in the depiction of the sash of the lower garment and the lotus held in the lower right hand. In both instances we see a style that is different from depictions in the rest of Southeast Asia. In Vietnam, the design is more stiff and symbolic. It moves away from a realistic style. Earlier bronze statuettes of Avalokiteśvara from Java, Sumatra and Thailand for example, also had lower garments with a herringbone pattern and a fabric flap, but the textiles were depicted in a more realistic manner (Image 10).

This artistic language will separate worshippers from the depicted figure as it is clear he is of a different world. In Thailand and Indonesia, we see a realistic style with how a fabric is draped as we shall see in the coming chapters.

Image 10. Example of a bronze with a more realistic style of dress from Peninsular Malaya. Drawing by Manisha Dayal.

3

Malaysia – Avalokiteśvara with the unfailing noose

Malaysia is a country that consists of two main parts, Peninsular Malaysia and Malaysian Borneo. However, these borders are relatively recent when compared with the Buddhist imagery that was produced in the region more than 1,000 years ago. A few different Avalokiteśvara images have been found in northern Peninsular Malaysia, but one in particular stands out due to its size and its surviving details. This is a statue of a specific form of the Bodhisattva Avalokiteśvara, known as Amoghapāśa Lokeśvara.

Amoghapāśa Lokeśvara is a manifestation of the Bodhisattva Avalokiteśvara who carries a *pāśa* or noose in order to rope in souls and save those who are lost and suffering. Just as in the previous images in this book, he can be identified as Avalokiteśvara due to the Buddha Amitābha in his headdress and as Amoghapāśa Lokeśvara because of the rope that he carries in one of his hands. Amoghapāśa means the unfailing noose, whereas Lokeśvara in another name for Avalokiteśvara, thus the name means Avalokiteśvara with the Unfailing Noose.

Amoghapāśa Lokeśvara has his origins in South Asia, but the first reference to this form of the Bodhisattva was in a text translated into Chinese in the *Amoghapāśa-dhāraṇī-sūtra* (The

Recitation of the Unfailing Noose) in 587 CE. This is not the only Buddhist text to express the merits of worshipping Amoghapāśa Lokeśvara, there are later versions such as the *Amoghapāśa kalparāja-sūtra*. This text describes how a ruler may use the text to become a *cakravatin* or a Universal Monarch, a person who rules with benevolence over the entire world.

Amoghapāśa Lokeśvara is described in these texts as being powerful and compassionate, but the text on its own is also beneficial. If a devotee fasts and then recites the *Amoghapāśa-dhāraṇī-sūtra* seven times, then he or she would have their karma cleansed and receive twenty blessings. The idea of karma is essential within Buddhism, and means action or deed. It is one of the main tenants of Buddhism and determines where a person will be reborn and in what form. This alone makes the text attractive to any devotee. It can also treat physical and psychological illnesses, making it a protective text. By reciting the text over medicine, such as melted butter or water, it will become more effective. For instance, resinous water could be used for sore eyes and sesame oil for ear aches.

This Malaysian Amoghapāśa Lokeśvara statue was found in an old open tin mine in the state of Perak (Image 11). The Bodhisattva had eight arms, but unfortunately one is now missing. The upper right hand holds a rosary and the hand directly below a staff. The lower right hand displays the gift-giving gesture. On the left side, we see a twisted rope in the upper hand. This represents the lasso that Amoghapāśa Lokeśvara uses to rope in individual souls in order to save them. The frontal left hand holds a lotus, with the flower

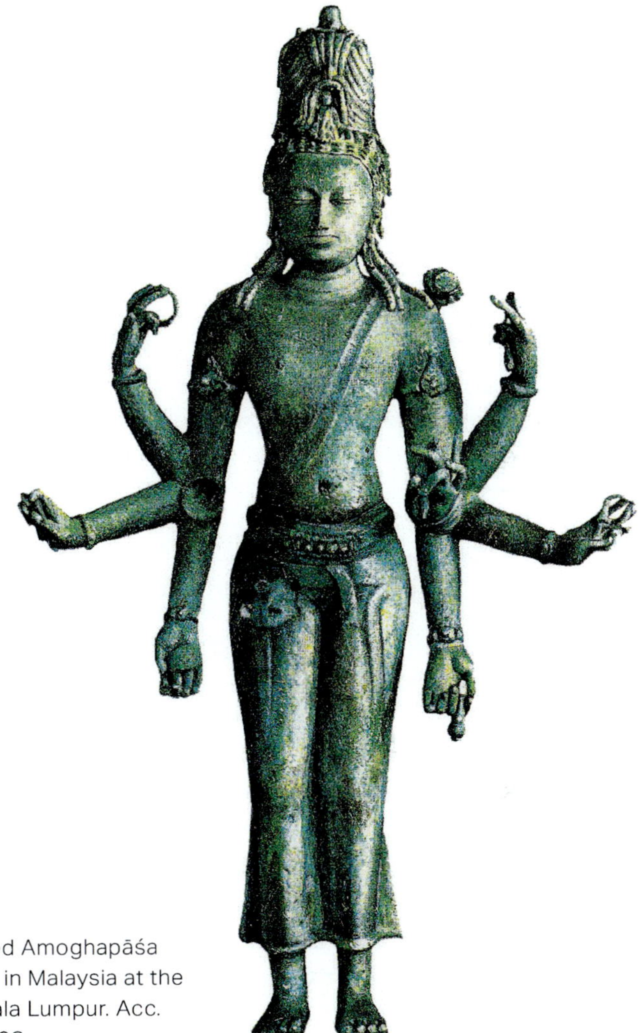

Image 11. Eight-armed Amoghapāśa Lokeśvara from Perak in Malaysia at the Muzium Negara in Kuala Lumpur. Acc. No. MN.BALAIB.40.2008.

visible by the left shoulder. The middle hand displays the fearlessness gesture and the lower left hand has the remains of a water vessel.

Amoghapāśa Lokeśvara has a tall headdress with a small niche for the Buddha Amitābha at the front. This type of headdress is quite unusual in the region, due to its height. A second unusual feature is the missing necklace. If Avalokiteśvara wears armbands and bracelets, he

What does the Bodhisattva's gesture mean?

A hand gesture or a mudrā can be shown with one or two hands. Avalokiteśvara has two popular styles of hand gestures in Southeast Asia, the gift-giving gesture (varada-mudrā) and the fearlessness gesture (abhaya-mudrā). The first of these is illustrated by the Bodhisattva having an open palm with the fingers pointing downwards (Image 18). This is the most common gesture for Avalokiteśvara and it illustrates his generosity. The second gesture is also an open palm, but here the fingers point upwards (Image 12). This is a calming gesture, which can reassure the worshipper.

normally also wears a necklace. The tiger skin around his hips has a similar face as the one seen on one of the gold statuettes from Sumatra, as seen in the following chapter. The head faces towards the Bodhisattva's left leg.

The attributes and the gestures of this statue illustrate the intent of the Buddhist texts describing this form of Avalokiteśvara.

The gesture of fearlessness, or the *abhaya-mudrā*, was first used in Buddhist art in depictions of the Historical Buddha, Śakyamuni (Image 12). This gesture spread with Buddhism and its art, but in Southeast Asia it is only used by Buddhas and Bodhisattvas in the Buddhist pantheon. The rosary can be used in the recitation of the text and the water vessel may contain water as a type of medicine. The rope refers of course to Amoghapāśa Lokeśvara's ability to rescue individual souls with

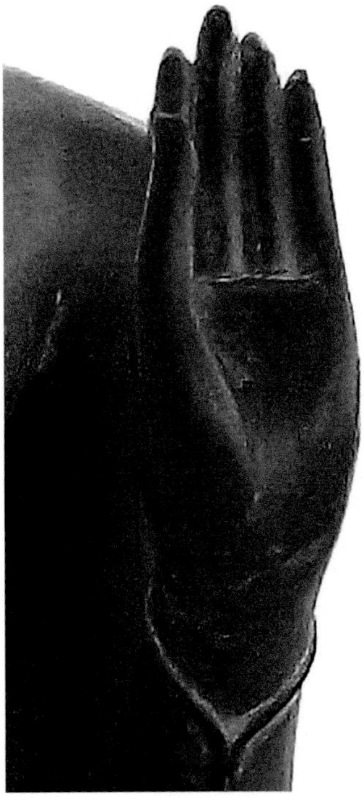

Image 12. Gesture of fearlessness.

his unfailing noose. Thus, the image is itself an illustration of the powerful text, just as the text is another form of expressing the power of this iconographic type.

Images of Amoghapāśa Lokeśvara have also been found on Java, Sulawesi, Sumatra and in Cambodia. Unlike the sorrowful Avalokiteśvara that we will look at in the chapter on Java, Amoghapāśa Lokeśvara was clearly popular across the region. The initial images of this specific iconographic form date to approximately the 800s CE, but the knowledge of this type of Avalokiteśvara did not disappear over time. We see instead depictions of Amoghapāśa Lokeśvara up until the end of the thirteenth century CE.

One bronze statuette of Amoghapāśa Lokeśvara can now be seen at the Museum Nasional Indonesia in Jakarta (Image 13).

The figure sits in a relaxed pose with one leg resting on the seat and fortunately all eight arms are intact. The upper right hand holds a rosary and the hand directly below displays the fearlessness gesture. The third hand from the top holds a twisted rope and the lower right hand displays the gesture of gift-giving. The upper left hand holds a manuscript and the hand below, a water vessel. The third left hand carries a three-pronged staff and the lower left hand is behind the body, but clearly holds a long-stemmed lotus. We can see the flower just above the left shoulder.

Image 13. Eight-armed seated Amoghapāśa Lokeśvara in the Museum Nasional, Jakarta. Acc. no. 603.

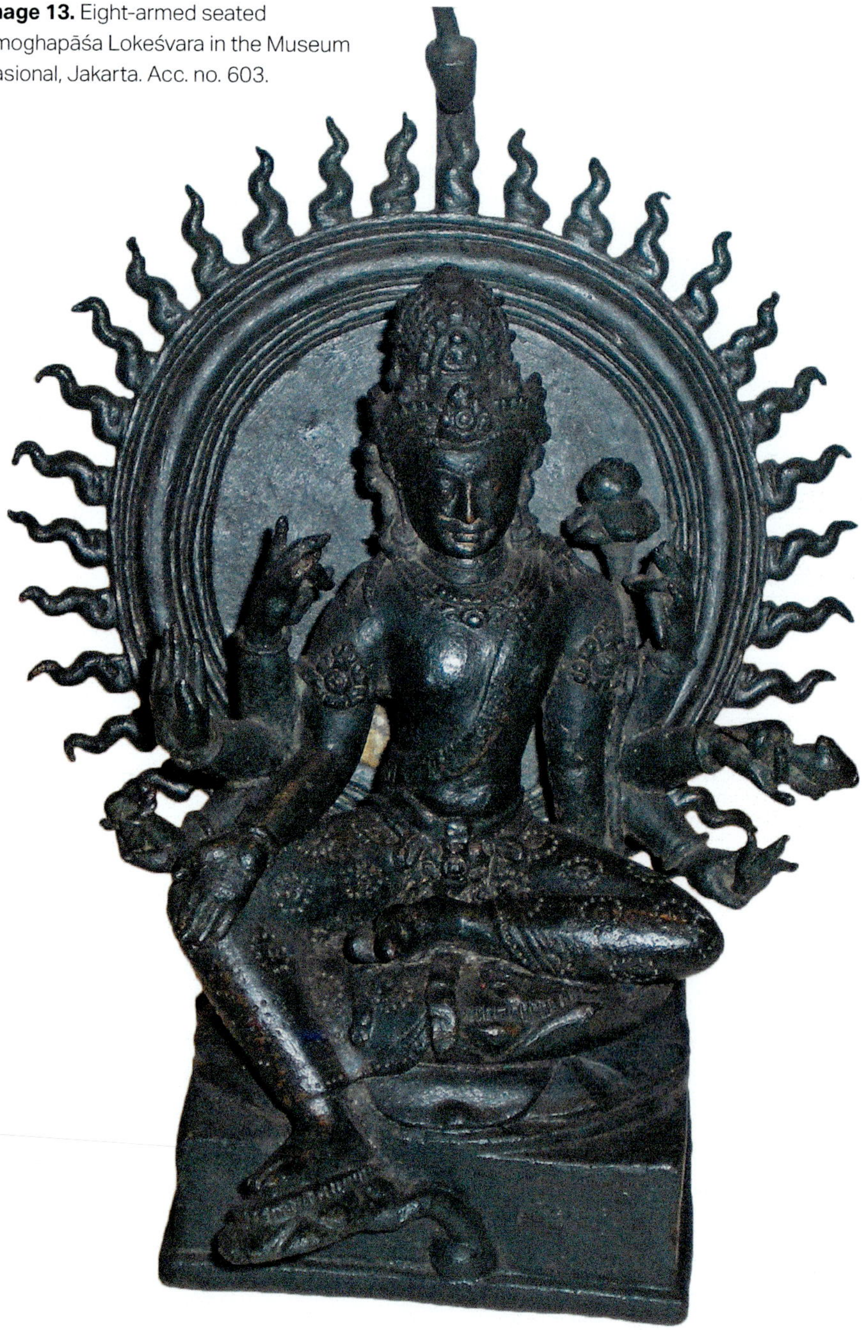

These are the same attributes and gestures as the Malaysian Amoghapāśa Lokeśvara displayed, just in different hands. The headdress also has another silhouette and the Buddha Amitabha is depicted in front of the headdress, rather than in a niche. The bronze statuette shows the Bodhisattva as sitting and the seat and back piece have survived as well. The amount of jewellery that the figure wears, a necklace, bracelets and armbands indicate that this bronze was produced during the Central Javanese period, likely in the late eighth or early ninth century CE.

One of the last depictions of Amoghapāśa Lokeśvara from the Buddhist period in Southeast Asia can be found among several bronze plaques produced in East Java in the late thirteenth century CE. Five of these plaques have survived until the present day. It shows Amoghapāśa Lokeśvara surrounded by his retinue of twelve figures as is described in another Buddhist text, *Amoghapāśa-sādhana*, written by the monk Śākyaśrībhadra (1127-1225).

According to the stories, Śākyaśrībhadra, became very sick during a visit to the Buddhist site, Bodh Gaya in northern India, and he began fasting as a way to cure himself. It was during this fast that he had a vision of the Bodhisattva Amoghapāśa Lokeśvara, along with his retinue. Once he was better he wrote down this vision, which became the *Amoghapāśa-sādhana*. The text itself was finalised by another monk, Vibhūticandra, before 1204, when both monks fled to Nepal.

It did not take long for this specific text to reach Java. Its influence can be seen in the five surviving bronze plaques, but also in the imagery from an East Javanese temple, Candi Jago, as well

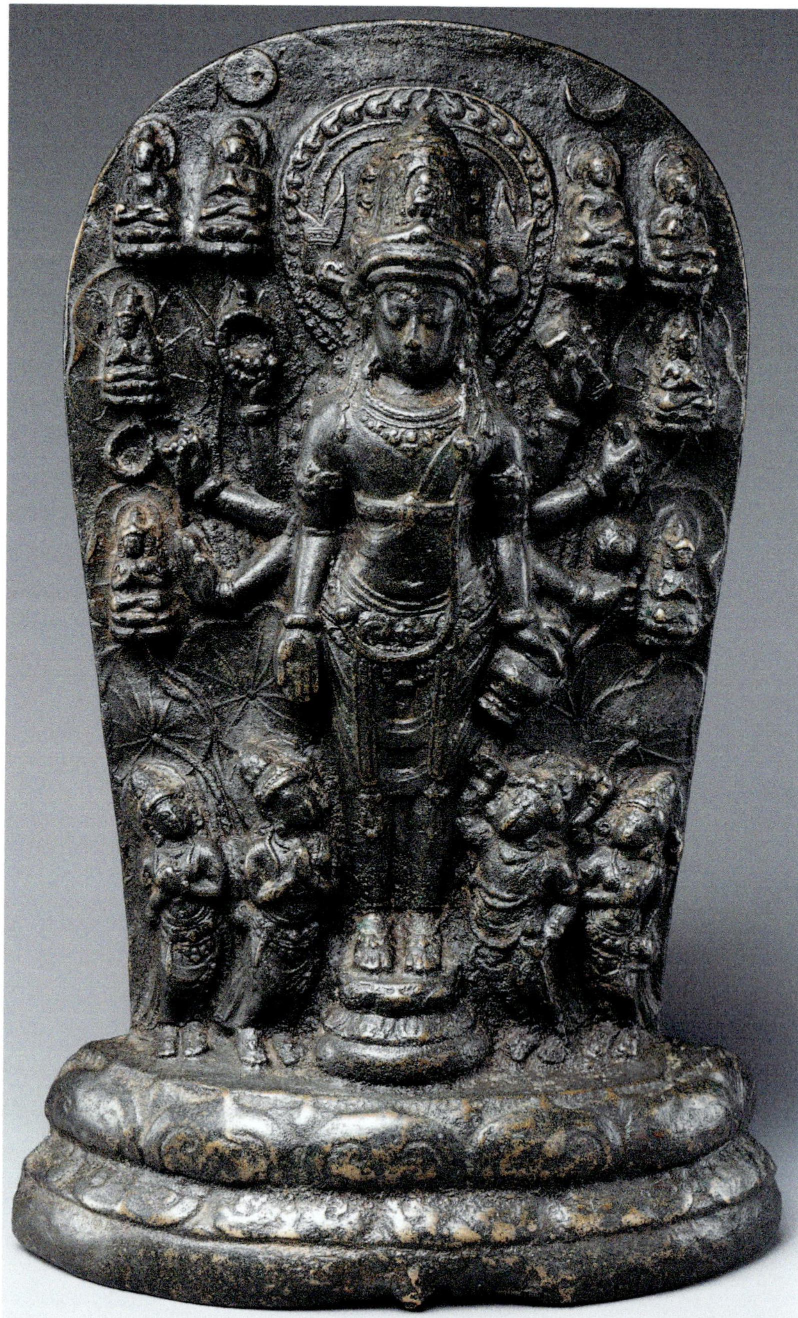

Image 14. Amoghapāśa Lokeśvara plaque in the Metropolitan Museum of Art, New York. Acc. no. 2014.517.

as in a large stone sculpture gifted to Sumatra by the then ruler of Java, Kṛtanagara, which helps us date these bronze plaques to the late thirteenth century CE.

One plaque is now in the Metropolitan Museum of Art in New York, USA (Image 14). Two of the other plaques are in Dutch museums and a fourth is in a museum in Berlin, Germany. This plaque illustrates Amoghapāśa Lokeśvara's attendants: Tārā, Sudhanakumāra, Hayagrīva and Bhṛkuṭī. They stand on either side of him and then there are the four Buddhas and their consorts floating in the air around the figure. Here we can see the Bodhisattva's attributes and hand gestures clearly. In his top right hand the Bodhisattva holds a rosary and in the hand below the famous noose or rope. The two lower right hands show the gestures of fearlessness and gift-giving. On the left side from the top he holds a book, a staff, a lotus and a water bottle.

On the backs of these plaques is also an inscription, rare among the Southeast Asian images of Avalokiteśvara (Image 15). This inscription first gives the Buddhist creed or the *ye dharma*, the importance of which is difficult to quantify in Buddhism. It is found inscribed in a myriad of places through the Buddhist world, including in Kedah, another state in Peninsular Malaysia. It consists of only a few lines that were spoken by one of the first monks that the Buddha converted after he had achieved enlightenment. These five monks were later travelling and encountered an ascetic, Śāriputra, who asked them about the Buddha's teaching. By simply hearing this description of the Buddha's teaching, or the *ye dharma*, Śāriputra was able to reach the first stage on the path to

Image 15. Back of Amoghapāśa Lokeśvara plaque with an inscription in the Metropolitan Museum of Art, New York. Acc. no. 2014.517.

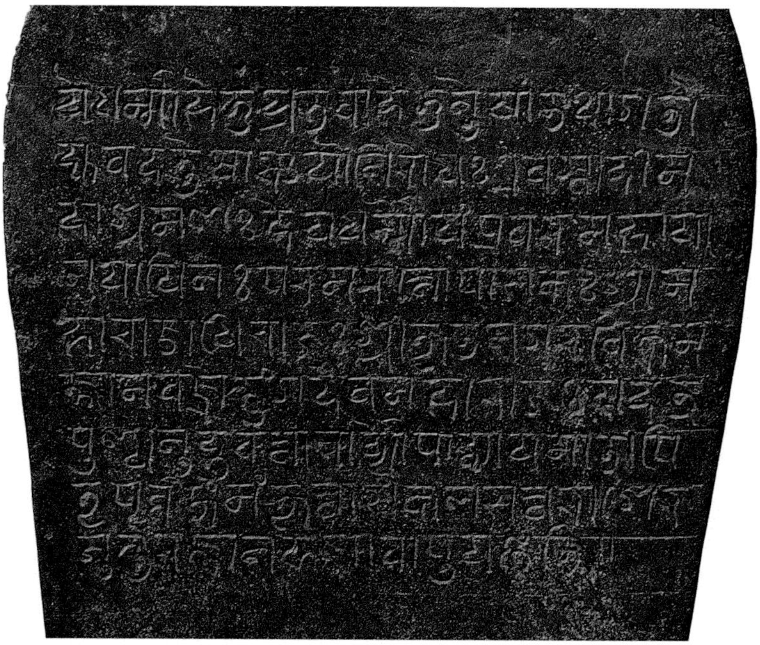

enlightenment. After the *ye dharma*, the inscription on the back of the plaque continues to identify the ruler Kṛtanagara as the donor of the plaques along with being the son and successor of Viṣṇuvardhana, the former ruler of East Java.

Thus, we find images of Amoghapāśa Lokeśvara in various locations in Southeast Asia, but they were also produced over several centuries, from the eighth century to the thirteenth century CE. The essential attribute of this iconographic form is the rope that the Bodhisattva uses to save souls, and it is present in each of these examples. From the different Buddhist texts, which describe Amoghapāśa Lokeśvara, we see him depicted as a powerful force for cleansing an individual person's karma, but who can also cure various illnesses and grant blessings. All very beneficial qualities for any devotee. We are fortunate that the Malaysian Amoghapāśa Lokeśvara survived until the present day. Only a few Avalokiteśvara images have been found in Malaysia, while Thailand, Cambodia and Java have left us a great many images to study. By this Malaysian Amoghapāśa Lokeśvara alone, we can see that there was a Buddhist community in Peninsular Malaysia and other remains show that it was particularly in the states of Kedah and Perak that this community flourished.

4

Sumatra – the golden Avalokiteśvaras

Sumatra is one of the many islands in Indonesia. It has – just as the other areas of Southeast Asia – a long history with Buddhism. Sumatra has lived in the shadows of the archaeological marvels of Java, such as Borobudur, and today it is best known for its wonderful wildlife. Yet, researchers continue to focus on Sumatra where the capital of the once powerful kingdom of Srivijaya is believed to have been located.

The name for this empire or polity comes from a stone inscription dated to 683 CE, which is now on display at the National Museum in Jakarta, Indonesia. The inscription speaks of a king who mounted an expedition by both land and sea and he was victorious. In the text he is described as bringing prosperity to Srivijaya.

Srivijaya appears to have waned as a power in 742 CE since they stopped sending emissaries to China. However, this was not the end of Buddhism on Sumatra, new power centres grew, and we have inscriptions from various locations on the island. Srivijaya was also mentioned in the writings of the Chinese monk Yijing, who visited Srivijaya on his way to India and once again as he was returning to China. On his return journey in 671 CE, he stayed in Srivijaya for two years, transcribing and translating Buddhist texts he had acquired in South Asia. He noted that there were 1,000 monks living at various monasteries in Srivijaya at the time. No evidence of such a developed area, which could have supported 1,000 monks, had been found from the Srivijayan time period. That was until the 1990s, when a neighbourhood of modern day Palembang was shown to have had an extensive network of canals and islands, indicating it had been home to a complex urban centre.

Different types of Buddhist images have been found at various sites on Sumatra. A few were even dragged from the Musi River near Palembang, further supporting that this was the location for the Srivijayan power centre. Among these images are several Avalokiteśvara bronze statuettes that fit into the pan-cultural response period before the seventh century CE, discussed in Chapter 1. But perhaps the two most memorable Avalokiteśvara images from Sumatra have a slightly later date and have a golden appearance. They were found at different locations on Sumatra and anyone who has had the opportunity to pick one of these statues up they remember their heaviness and solidity even years later. Add to this their golden appearance, these images easily become unforgettable. They each show Avalokiteśvara in his standing four-armed form. Both figures stand in *tribhaṅga*, which means that the body is bent in order to create an s-shape.

The idea of compassion may be illustrated in different ways. It can take the form of visual acceptance, where the Bodhisattva has calm facial features illustrating an inner peace, just as we see in the image above (Image 16). Here,

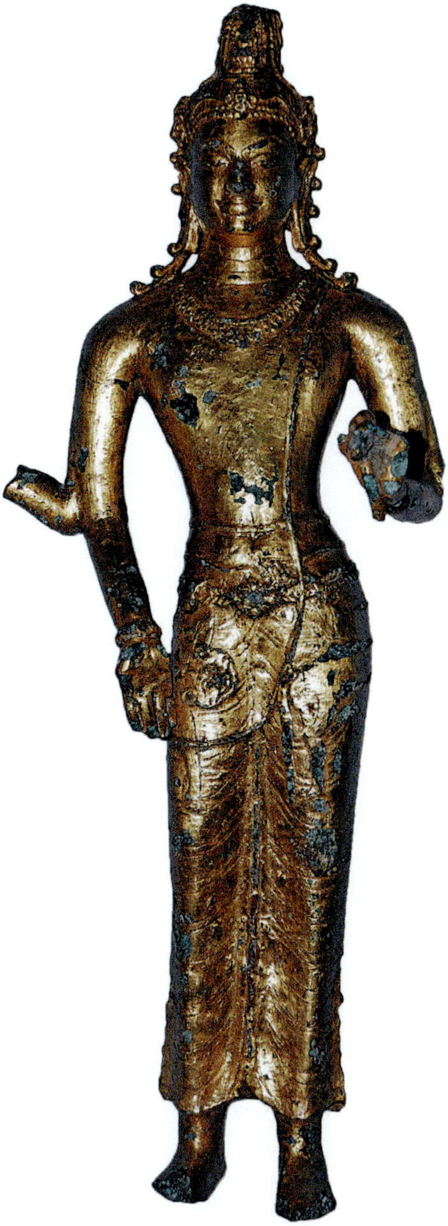

Avalokiteśvara has his eyes closed in meditation and has a beneficent smile on his lips. His hair is pulled up into a short headdress with the Buddha Amitabha seated at the front. Some hair tresses escape the headdress and fall in curls down on both shoulders. The Bodhisattva wears quite an elaborate necklace, but plain bracelets and no armbands. The sacred thread hangs from his left shoulder and crosses the body below the right hip. A tiger skin is tied around the hips. We can see the head of the tiger on the right hip and it faces to the left. The lower garment is pulled up in between the legs, which is illustrated by the herringbone pattern incised into the metal. While two of the arms are significantly damaged it is clear that the lower right hand displays the gift-giving gesture and the lower left hand holds the stem of what once represented a lotus.

The second Sumatran statue is only slightly smaller than the first

Image 16. Four-armed bejewelled golden Avalokiteśvara from Sumatra.

and is missing its feet (Image 17). Avalokiteśvara's face is unusual as he has his eyes open and he also has a small smile on his lips. He does not wear any jewellery except a headband with a flower at the front. Avalokiteśvara's headdress has a niche, but the Buddha Amitābha is now missing. Just as in the previous statue, the headdress has curled locks falling down over the shoulders.

This golden image was found near Jambi on the east coast of Sumatra. Its lower garment is slightly different from the first statuette. Instead of being pulled up in the centre it is fastened to the left side which is indicated by the incised lines in the metal. All the Bodhisattva's attributes are missing, but he displays the *varada-mudrā* with his lower right hand. Due to the shape of what remains of the hands, it is likely that the upper right hand held a rosary and the lower left hand a lotus.

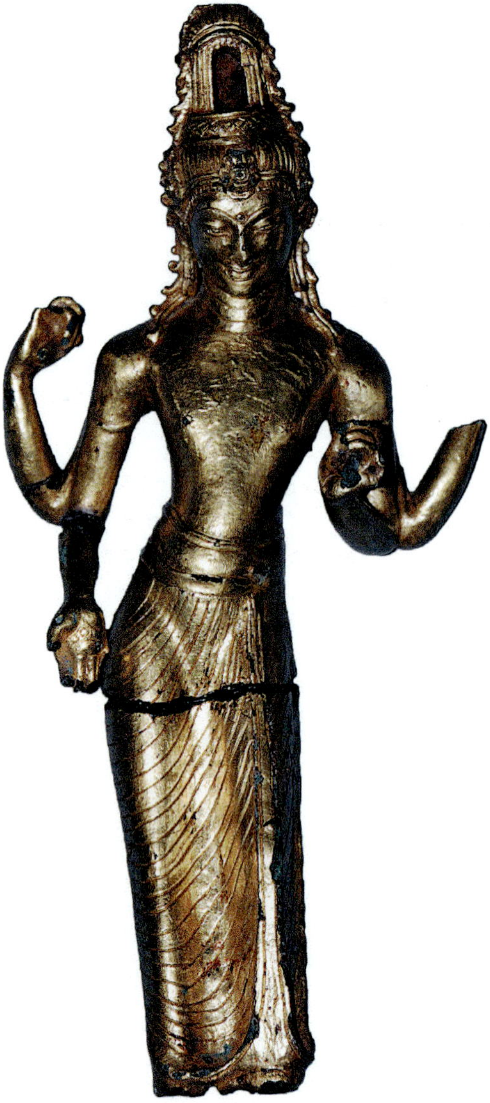

Image 17. Four-armed Avalokiteśvara with a hollow niche in the headdress from Sumatra.

Sumatra was once known as Swarnadwīpa or Island of Gold, which is certainly sustained by these two golden statues. Even though there is no inscription describing why these images were made, or by whom, we can speculate who sponsored the production of these golden statues. It may have been a merchant who had managed to accumulate quite a bit of wealth. We know that travelling merchants were important in the spread of Buddhism to Southeast Asia and one of Avalokiteśvara's many powers was protecting ships from storms. A second possibility is a local ruler who funded different types of Buddhist works. The statues may have been cast as a tribute, but more likely they were made as a way to gain merit. An example of such a sponsorship is seen in the foundation of a monastery by the Sumatran ruler, Bālaputra, in Nalanda in Bihar, north-eastern India. In a Nalanda inscription, dating to 850-860 CE, the local Pala ruler granted the ruler of Swarnadwīpa the right to build a Buddhist monastery. The Pala ruler, Devapaladeva, also granted five villages to the upkeep of the monastery.

We saw another example of a ruler funding Buddhist works in the previous chapter of the Malaysian Amoghapāśa Lokeśvara. The Javanese ruler, Kṛtanagara, commissioned at least five bronze plaques of Amoghapāśa Lokeśvara and his retinue towards the end of the thirteenth century CE. The inscription on the back of the plaques describes that any merit made from producing the plaques should be for the good of all creatures. There are various ways of gaining merit in Buddhism, but funding the production of images is a common way for lay people to gain merit.

Merit comes from performing good deeds, but the most fruitful are those deeds performed in connection with the Buddha, the Law or the Monastic community. Among these is the production of images, the spread of Buddhist texts and teachings as well as funding the Monastic community in some way. Any merit that is accrued by you can be given to someone else, including a deceased person, and it is all done by a mental wish. The production of these golden statues of Avalokiteśvara would certainly have gained their patrons merit.

5

Borneo – the Sambas hoard

The island of Borneo is home to three separate countries: Brunei, part of Malaysia and Kalimantan (a part of Indonesia). The earliest dated inscriptions from Indonesia were actually found in north-eastern Borneo, nevertheless, finds of historical artefacts on the island are quite limited making the Sambas hoard exceptional. It was discovered in the 1940s when a farmer was digging in the ground outside of the town of Sambas in south-western Borneo. The hoard consists of nine figures and a bronze vessel. This treasure of images made in gold, silver and bronze was kept contained within an earthenware vessel that had been completely buried. We can imagine the sound a tool must have made as it broke the vessel. A jarring sound after having worked with the soil day in and day out. Reaching down to see the origin of the sound, someone discovered a cache of Buddhist images.

There is no record as to what happened to the discoverer, but we may hope that this buried treasure gave him and his family some security over the coming years. The images, along with the bronze vessel, were collected by a Singaporean historian, Tan Yeok Seong. He eventually sold it to Percy Thomas Brooke Sewell, who donated the entire treasure to the British Museum, London, in 1956, where it is now on display.

As part of this hoard, we discover four statuettes of the Bodhisattva Avalokiteśvara in silver and gold. We quickly find two similarities between these four images when we examine the hand gestures and the attributes. All these figures display the gift-giving gesture (*varada-mudrā*) and each one holds a lotus (Image 18). The gift-giving gesture is the most common type of gesture displayed by Avalokiteśvara in Southeast Asia. It shows an open palm with the fingers pointing downwards. The gesture symbolises the generosity, sincerity and the compassion of the Buddhas and Bodhisattvas.

Each of the four lotuses carried by the Avalokiteśvara statuettes in this hoard has a different style. One is in bloom, two are in bud form and the final lotus is a bud beginning to blossom. The lotus is an essential attribute in Mahayana Buddhism since it represents the balance within the religion. This ethereal flower resting on the surface of the tranquil water actually has its roots in the deep, dark mud at the bottom. The plant is a living illustration of how we cannot know happiness without suffering and that despite our origins, we may all achieve more ethereal qualities in our path towards enlightenment.

A lotus is used in a description of a Bodhisattva from the *Ratnagotravibhāga* which explains the Buddha-nature present in all beings:

> As a lotus flower, though it grows in water, is not polluted by the water,
> So he, though born in the world, is not polluted by worldly dharmas (Conze *et al.* 2014: 130).

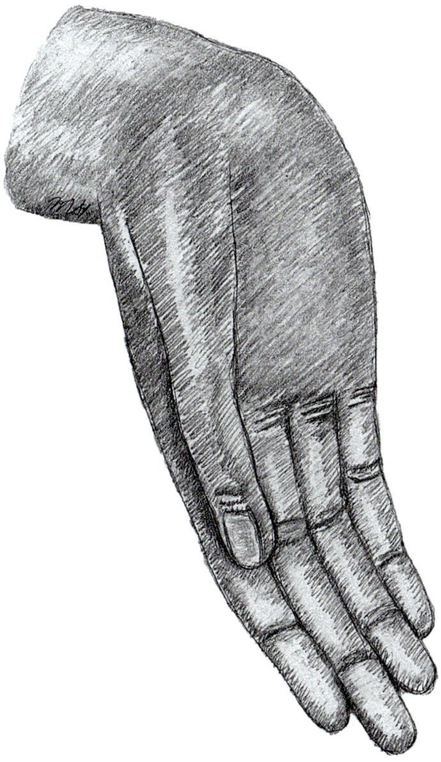

Image 18 (above). The gift-giving gesture. Drawing by Manisha Dayal.

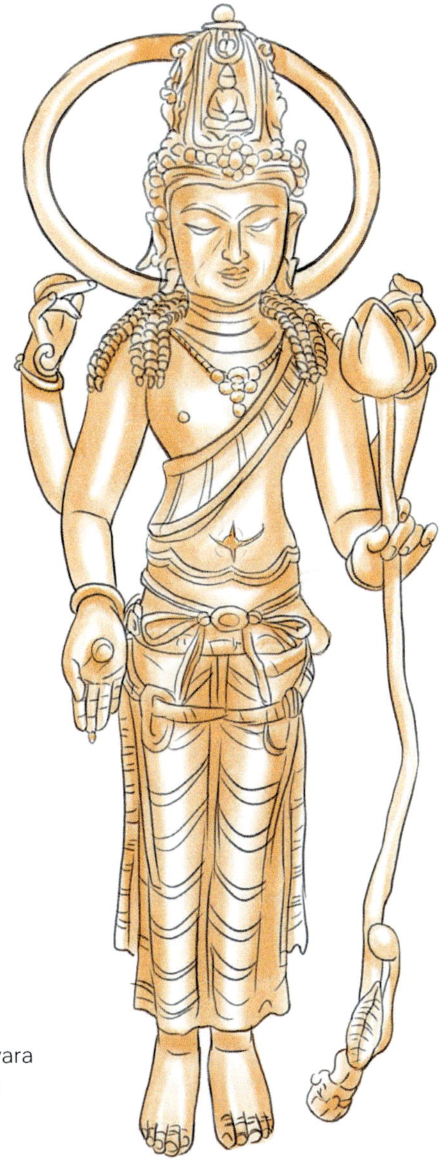

Image 19 (right). Golden four-armed Avalokiteśvara with a circular halo from the Sambas hoard in the British Museum, London. Acc. no. 1956,0725.4. Drawing by Jenni Söderlund.

The first beautiful gold statuette in the Sambas hoard shows Avalokiteśvara with four arms (Image 19). We can clearly see the Buddha Amitābha in the Bodhisattva's headdress. On either side of Avalokiteśvara's head fall braids of hair over his shoulders, referencing his earlier imagery showing him as an ascetic. On his right side, Avalokiteśvara holds a rosary in his upper hand and he displays the gift-giving gesture with his lower hand. In his open palm is a small pearl that represents the *cintāmaṇi* or the wish-fulfilling jewel. On his left side he holds a book in his upper hand and a long-stemmed lotus in his lower hand. This lotus is a separate piece from the figure and can be thread through Avalokiteśvara's lower left hand.

The combination of the gesture and these three attributes for this statuette is quite common among Javanese bronzes from the Buddhist period in Java. They speak to Avalokiteśvara's specific qualities and actions. The gift-giving gesture is often associated with the Bodhisattva's visit to Avici hell, where he let water flow from the palms of his hands and feet, quenching the thirst of the hungry ghosts. The rosary is used in Buddhist meditation along with the recitation of mantras and as mentioned above, the lotus symbolises the duality within Buddhism.

This statuette shows Avalokiteśvara in his princely form. He wears a diadem on his head, a pendant necklace and bracelets. A sacred thread (*yajñopavīta*) is draped over Avalokiteśvara's torso and is decorated with the same textile pattern as the lower garment – a double line design. The sides of the lower garment are pulled up and fastened by sashes, which creates the swallow's tail effect at the bottom.

Only one of the Avalokiteśvara images in this hoard has two arms, a form of Avalokiteśvara examined in the Introduction. Depicting Avalokiteśvara with four arms became popular by the 700s in Southeast Asia and we can see one of the earliest carved in stone at the Buddhist caves in Maharashtra, India. The hoard's two-armed Avalokiteśvara shows him displaying the gift-giving gesture and holding a lotus bud in his left hand (Image 20). The lower garment is decorated with an indented star-shaped pattern, which was likely added once the statuette had been removed from its cast.

We see the same type of pattern on the four-armed Avalokiteśvara that has a tall back piece finishing in three prongs (Image 21). The top of the headdress also ends in three prongs.

The use of the three-pronged flame top in the headdress is an unusual feature for Avalokiteśvara statuettes from Southeast Asia. The only other example of this flame-shape can be seen in a Javanese Avalokiteśvara bronze, which is now in the Johnson Museum of Art, Cornell University, the United States of America. However, in this case the three-pronged flame is at the top of the bronze's back piece and not the Bodhisattva's headdress.

The use of this type of flat-leaf flames along the frame of the hollow back piece is also an unusual feature in Indonesian images. Yet, the plain circular halo attached to the figure's shoulders is a typical Central Javanese feature. In his upper

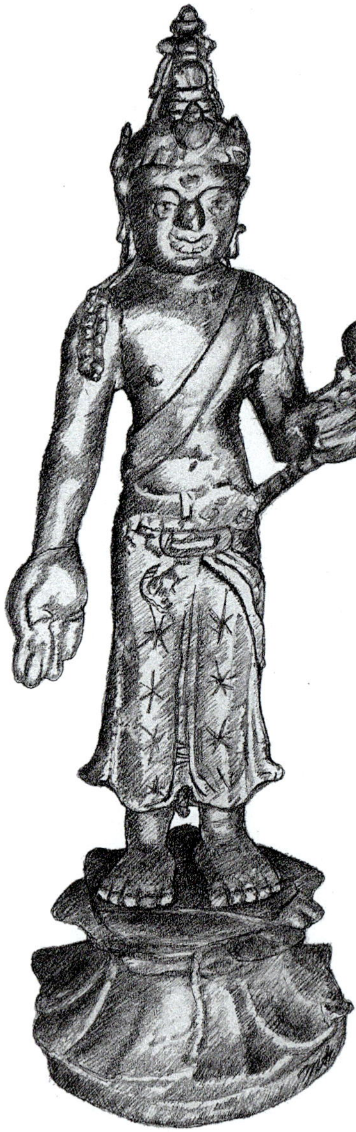

Image 20. Two-armed Avalokiteśvara from the Sambas hoard in the British Museum, London. Acc. no. 1956,0725.6. Drawing by Manisha Dayal.

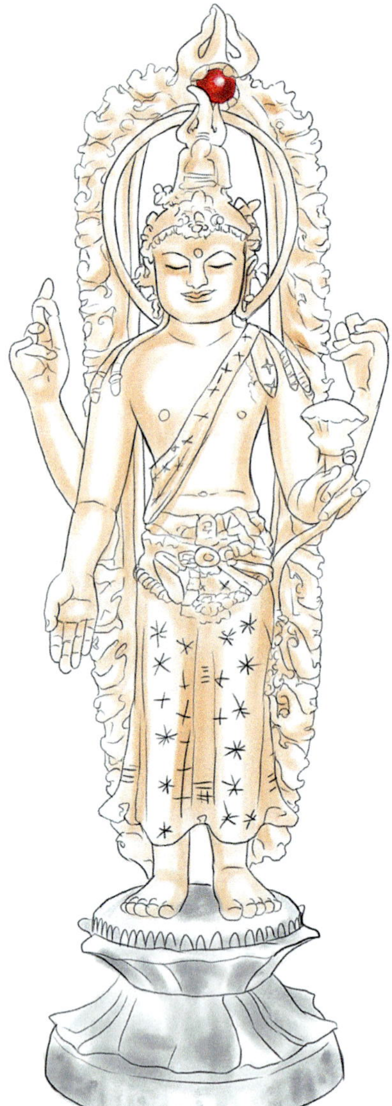

Image 21. Four-armed Avalokiteśvara with indented star pattern on the lower garment from the Sambas hoard in the British Museum, London. Acc. no. 1956,0725.5. Drawing by Jenni Söderlund.

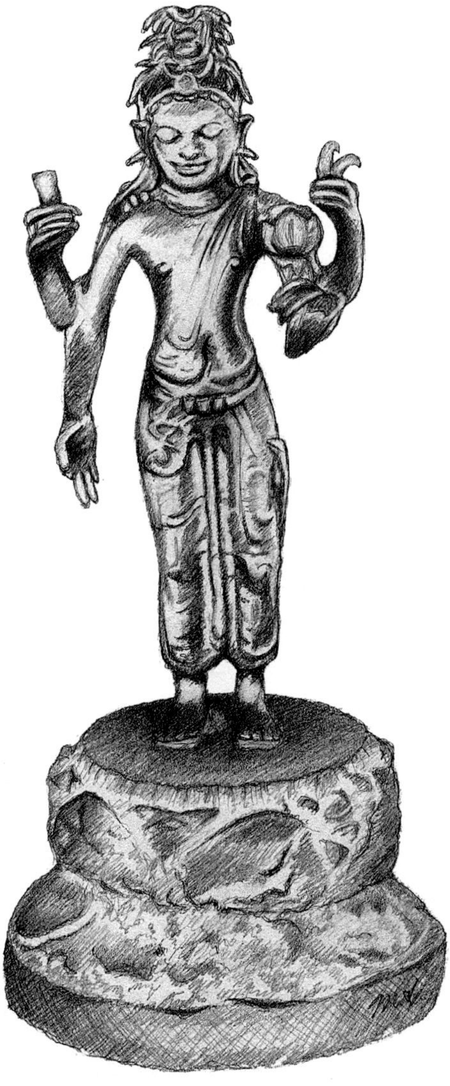

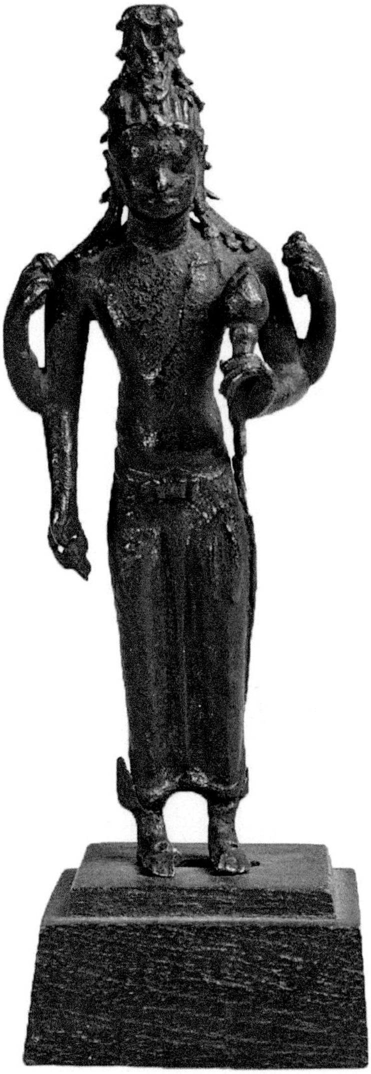

Image 22. Four-armed silver Avalokiteśvara from the Sambas hoard in the British Museum, London. Acc. no. 1956,0725.9. Drawing by Manisha Dayal.

Image 23. Four-armed Avalokiteśvara found at Borobudur and now at the Volkenkunde Museum, Leiden. Acc. no. RV-1403-1841.

right hand, Avalokiteśvara holds a rosary and displays the gift-giving gesture with his lower right hand. In the upper left hand he holds a book and in the lower hand a lotus with its stem attached to the left hip.

The fourth Avalokiteśvara statuette in the Sambas hoard shows him with four arms (Image 22). He has a flat rectangular headdress with the Buddha Amitābha seated in front. He does not have any jewellery, but he has a sacred thread in the form of a sash. In his upper right hand he holds a manuscript and he displays the gift-giving gesture with his lower right hand. On his left side he holds a three-pronged staff in his upper hand and a lotus in his lower hand. A tiger skin is tied around the Bodhisattva's hips. Avalokiteśvara stands on a round lotus base.

An almost identical image to the four-armed silver Avalokiteśvara can be found at the Volkenkunde Museum in Leiden, the Netherlands (Image 23). This second statuette was actually found inside the top stupa at Borobudur in Central Java. Quite a distance from where the Sambas hoard was found. Yet, if we examine both of these silver statuettes we see the same type of tiger skin around the hips and the same style of headdress.

The important thing about these two silver statuettes is that they can easily travel. They could simply be placed in a pocket and off they would go. Considering the strong similarity between these two statuettes, it is possible that they were made at the same time and by the same workshop. However, we still do not know where this workshop could have been located.

There is a difference in these two silver statuettes' attributes. The Sambas silver figure holds a book in his upper right hand and the remains of a three-pronged staff in his upper left hand. The Volkenkunde Avalokiteśvara holds a rosary or a three-pronged staff in his upper right hand and a book in his upper left hand, switching the sides for these attributes. The three-pronged staff can be interpreted in different ways. In some cases, it represents the three jewels of Buddhism: the Buddha, the Dharma and the Sangha. It may also represent the staff used by wandering monks.

The Sambas hoard and Buddhist texts

None of these statuettes carry an inscription, but two sheets of silver with an inscribed text were found with the hoard. The inscribed text is an excerpt of the vow of the Bodhisattva Samantabhadra, known as the *Bhadracarī*. The vow is to worship all the Buddhas and seek enlightenment for the benefit of all sentient beings. This Buddhist text was originally written before the fifth century CE and can be seen illustrated on the fourth level of Borobudur in Central Java (Image 24).

> Filled with faith, I honor with my body, speech and mind
> All the Lions among Men without exception
> Who abide in all three times,
> In the world with its ten directions (Osto 2010: 9).

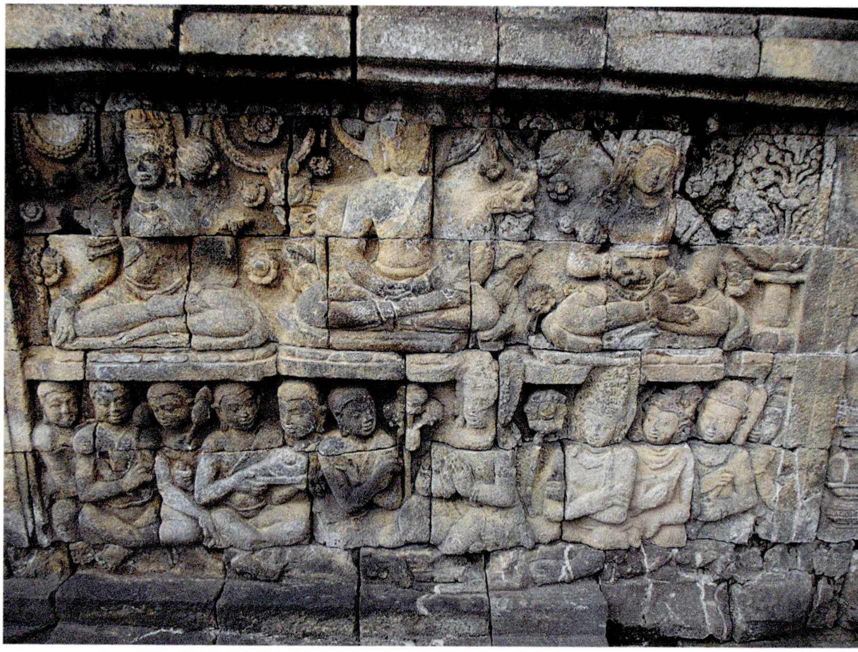

Image 24. Relief from the fourth level of Borobudur illustrating the *Bhadracarī*.

The Bodhisattva Avalokiteśvara is not mentioned directly in this text, however, he is repeatedly depicted in groups of Bodhisattvas in the *Bhadracarī* reliefs on Borobudur. It is also important to remember that Avalokiteśvara made this vow, just as Samantabhadra, as a Bodhisattva. As described in the early Buddhist text, the *Sukhāvatīvyūha-sūtra*, Avalokiteśvara can teach the correct Dharma or Law at the appropriate time. He has the wisdom of enlightenment and does not make mistakes. This vow is part of what makes Avalokiteśvara a symbol of compassion since he understands that all sentient beings suffer, and he wishes to aid them in their path to end their suffering.

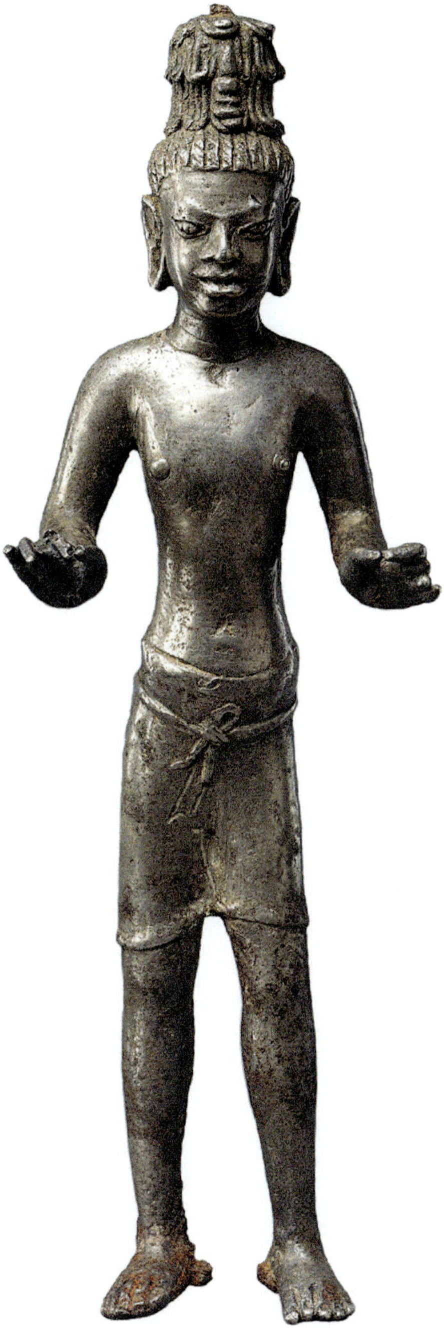

Why would someone bury images?

The Sambas hoard is not the only cache of Buddhist images found in Southeast Asia. This is actually how most statuettes are encountered in Java, often by a farmer digging in his fields. The largest cache of images in Southeast Asia was found in Prakhon Chai, Buriram province, in Thailand. It is rumoured to have held 53 statuettes, but likely contained even more than that as such images are easily transported away. One of the Prakhon Chai hoard's statuettes is now on display at the Metropolitan Museum of Art, New York (Image 25).

In the case of the Prakhon Chai hoard, the bronzes were wrapped in cloth and then buried in a stone-covered burial pit. Thus, burying images was not unheard of at the time. These statuettes were buried in connection with a temple which was turned from being Buddhist to

Image 25. Two-armed Maitreya from Prakhon Chai hoard in the Metropolitan Museum of Art, New York. Acc. no. 1994.51.

Hindu. However, neither the Sambas hoard, nor the statuettes unearthed in caches in Java, were found in connection with a temple. The burial of such images could have been used to consecrate the ground, but considering that no temple structures have been discovered near these caches the burial was likely not used in this manner. A consecrated image cannot simply be thrown away, but needs to be treated with reverence. They may be included in the walls or the interior of a stupa in a Buddhist temple, they can be buried in a river or clearly buried in the ground.

We are no closer to understanding why these metal statuettes and a bronze incense burner were buried together on Borneo. All the images are Buddhist, indicating that they were previously collected by a Buddhist or possibly a family. It is unlikely the Sambas hoard was buried in order to consecrate the ground, instead the pieces were buried as a means of protecting them. However, the styles of the different images indicate that they were made over a period of time, at least 100 years, and by different workshops. Yet, it is due to caches, such as the Sambas treasure or the Prakhon Chai hoard, that we have the large number of metal statuettes from 1,000 years ago in Southeast Asia.

6

Java – the sorrowful Avalokiteśvara

The island of Java in Indonesia may appear to have been quite isolated from outside influence over 1,000 years ago, but was actually a very active part of the Maritime Silk Route. Java's power centre was located in Central Java from 750-930 CE.

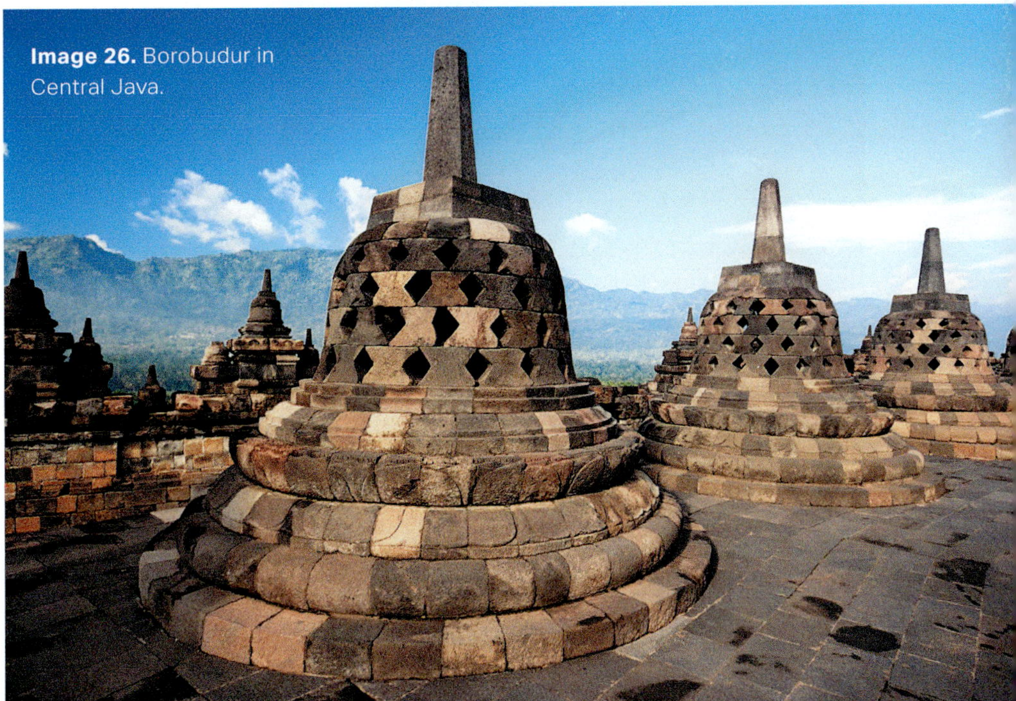

Image 26. Borobudur in Central Java.

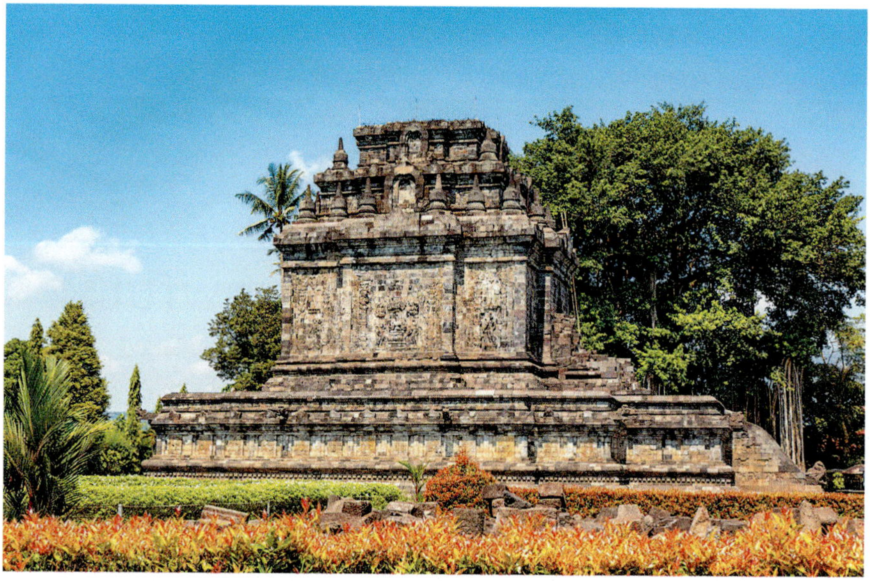

Image 27. Candi Mendut in Central Java.

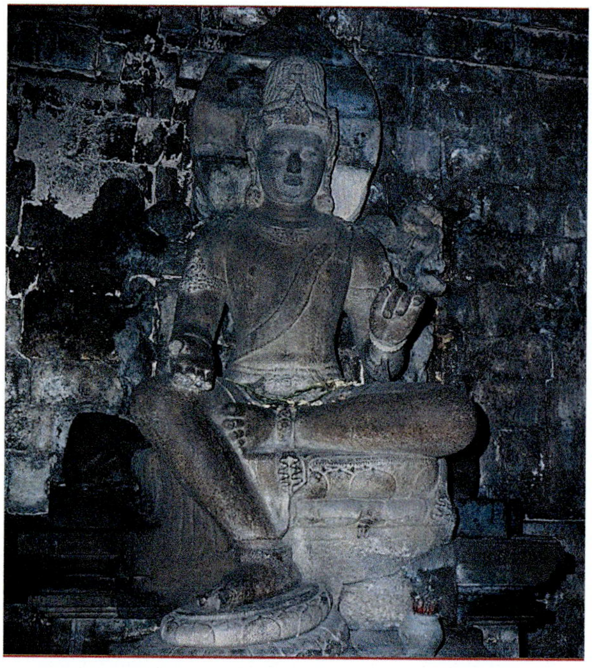

Image 28. Two-armed seated Avalokiteśvara inside Candi Mendut.

It was during this time that the astounding Borobudur (Image 26) was designed and constructed, as well as the Hindu temple known as Prambanan.

A second example of a Buddhist monument from the Central Javanese period can be seen in the Mendut village outside of city of Yogyakarta. The temple, Candi Mendut, is a short climb up to the entrance of the temple and once inside a visitor can easily be overwhelmed by the large size of the statues in that limited space (Image 27).

Facing the visitor is the Buddha who has his hands together in the gesture known as the Turning-of-the-Wheel, symbolising the point when he began to teach the Buddhist Law. On the Buddha's right-hand side, we can see Avalokiteśvara, impressive with the intricate jewellery design and compassionate facial features (Image 28). On the Buddha's left-hand side sits a second Bodhisattva. The combination of these three figures is referred to as a triad and is a common depiction in Buddhist art in India as well as in Java.

The large Avalokiteśvara statue displays the gift-giving gesture with his right hand that rests on the inside of his right knee. The attribute in the left hand is now missing. The right foot rests on a lotus, emerging from the dais and the left leg rests on the double lotus seat. The back piece has *makaras* facing outwards on either side of the Bodhisattva's shoulders. *Makaras* are a mythical animal often seen depicted in Javanese art on temples or in connection with thrones (Images 29 and 30).

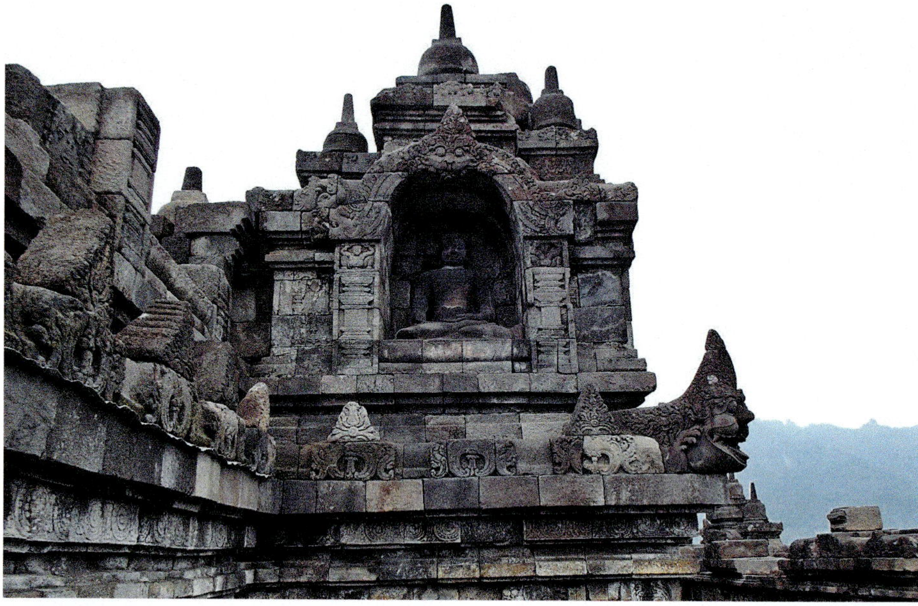

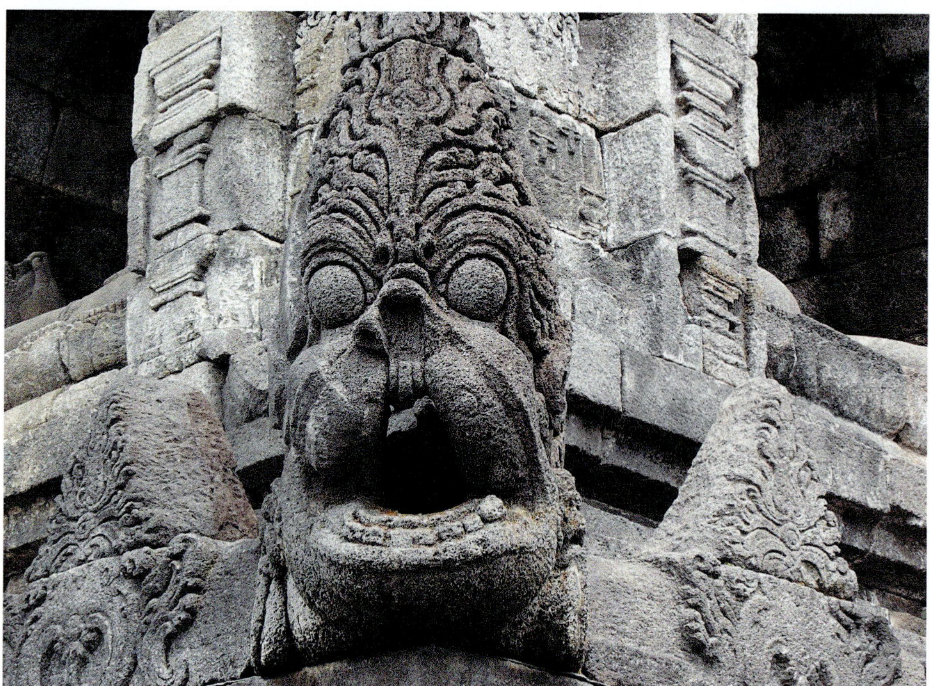

Image 29. Silhouette of a makara at Borobudur in Central Java.

Image 30. Close up of a makara drain spout at Prambanan in Central Java.

Below the *makaras* on the sides of the Candi Mendut throne are *vyālakas* standing on elephants. *Vyālakas* are also mythical creatures and are depicted as horned lions. This type of back piece with the combination of *makaras*, *vyālakas* and elephants is at times referred to as a 'royal throne'. It is used inside the Mendut temple, as well as a few times on Borobudur in connection with reliefs of the Buddha, Avalokiteśvara and the Buddha of the Future – Maitreya. One example of the use of the royal throne was the *Bhadracarī* relief from the fourth level included in the previous chapter (Image 24).

Yet, this time period did not just give us stone temples, but hundreds of bronze statuettes produced in a variety of workshops throughout the area. These bronze images show Avalokiteśvara in a myriad of forms, with different back pieces and bases. This vast variety of imagery shows that there were many bronze casters working to produce images, not just a few. The Javanese people must have truly appreciated these statuettes in order to support their production to this extent.

In many of these images, Avalokiteśvara is seated, which is a popular way to depict him in Java. However, in the rest of Southeast Asia, Avalokiteśvara is almost always depicted as standing. This is why a specific type of Avalokiteśvara image, the sorrowful Avalokiteśvara, can only be found in Java from 750-1100 CE.

The sorrowful Avalokiteśvara image clearly illustrates the Bodhisattva's compassion, the quality for which he is known. The Bodhisattva supports his head with his upper right hand and is a way of illustrating Avalokiteśvara's compassion

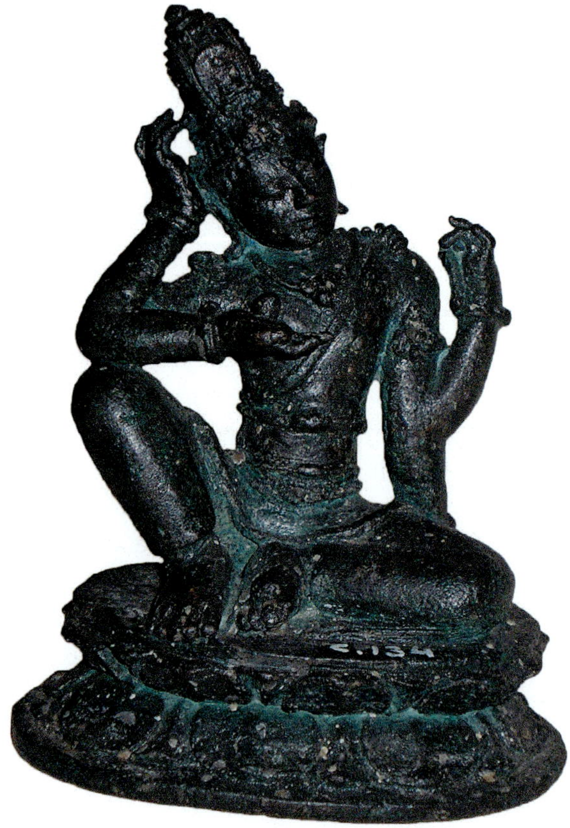

Image 31. Four-armed sorrowful Avalokiteśvara in the Museum Nasional, Jakarta. Acc. no. c.134.

over the suffering of sentient beings. In several of these statuettes, Avalokiteśvara is shown holding a wish-fulfilling jewel. It demonstrates a link to Sukhāvatī paradise, the home of the Buddha Amitābha. It can give whatever you wish for, including cure illnesses and manifest food. Certainly, a beneficial gem to have.

One statuette was found in Boyali in Central Java and is now at the National Museum in Jakarta (Image 31). We can easily identify this bronze as Avalokiteśvara, due to the Buddha figure at the front of the headdress. The Bodhisattva has four arms and uses his upper right hand to support his head. The lower right hand holds a wish-fulfilling jewel in front of the chest. The upper left hand holds a palm-leaf manuscript and the lower left hand rests on the lotus seat. Avalokiteśvara sits with both his feet resting next to each other on the oval double lotus seat and the right knee supports the lower right hand.

There are many stories that illustrate Avalokiteśvara's compassion. One speaks of the time he had visited hell, where he had saved all the suffering beings, and when he returned to his home on Mount Potalaka he saw that all the places in hell had once again been filled with suffering souls. He became so distraught that his head split into several pieces, but the Buddha Amitābha managed to reconstruct his head.

In the 1900s, this gesture has been interpreted as illustrating Avalokiteśvara being pensive, in part inspired by Auguste Rodin's *The Thinker*. However, the gesture of supporting the head in one hand is derived from Indian theatre and dance where gestures are used to portray various emotions. In this system of story-telling, supporting your head with one of your hands signifies that you are illustrating sorrow. The same gesture is used in the Buddhist caves of Maharashtra. There you can see a monk sitting in sorrow, leaning his head in his hand, after the death of the Buddha.

A small silver statuette of the sorrowful Avalokiteśvara is now at the Rijksmuseum in Amsterdam (Image 32). The Buddha Amitābha sits in front of the headdress and Avalokiteśvara wears a three-pronged diadem. We see the Bodhisattva glancing down towards the wish-fulfilling jewel in his lower left hand, possibly thinking about the suffering in the world. The upper right hand gently touches the leaning head

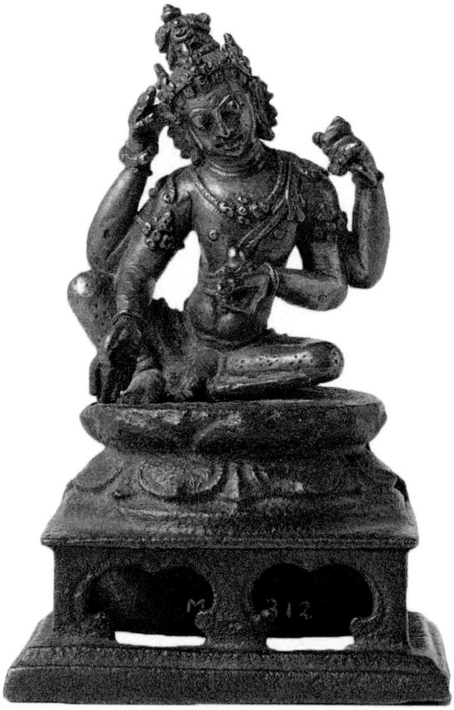

Image 32. Four-armed sorrowful Avalokiteśvara in the Rijksmuseum, Amsterdam. Acc. no. MAK 312.

and the lower right hand displays the gift-giving gesture. The upper left hand holds a palm-leaf manuscript.

The sorrowful gesture, where one hand supports the leaning head, is often seen in connection with the gift-giving gesture and a manuscript in Java. A bronze that shows a similar body silhouette to the Rijksmuseum sorrowful Avalokiteśvara is now at the Volkenkunde Museum in Leiden, the Netherlands (Image 33).

In this bronze, the Buddha Amitābha cannot be determined in the headdress. However, as the sorrowful gesture is only used for Avalokiteśvara bronze depictions in Java we can confidently say that this is Avalokiteśvara. He sits with both feet next to each other on the top of the lotus seat. The back piece has a parasol that extends out over the seated figure. The back piece consists of a herringbone frame with foliage along the rim. Avalokiteśvara's

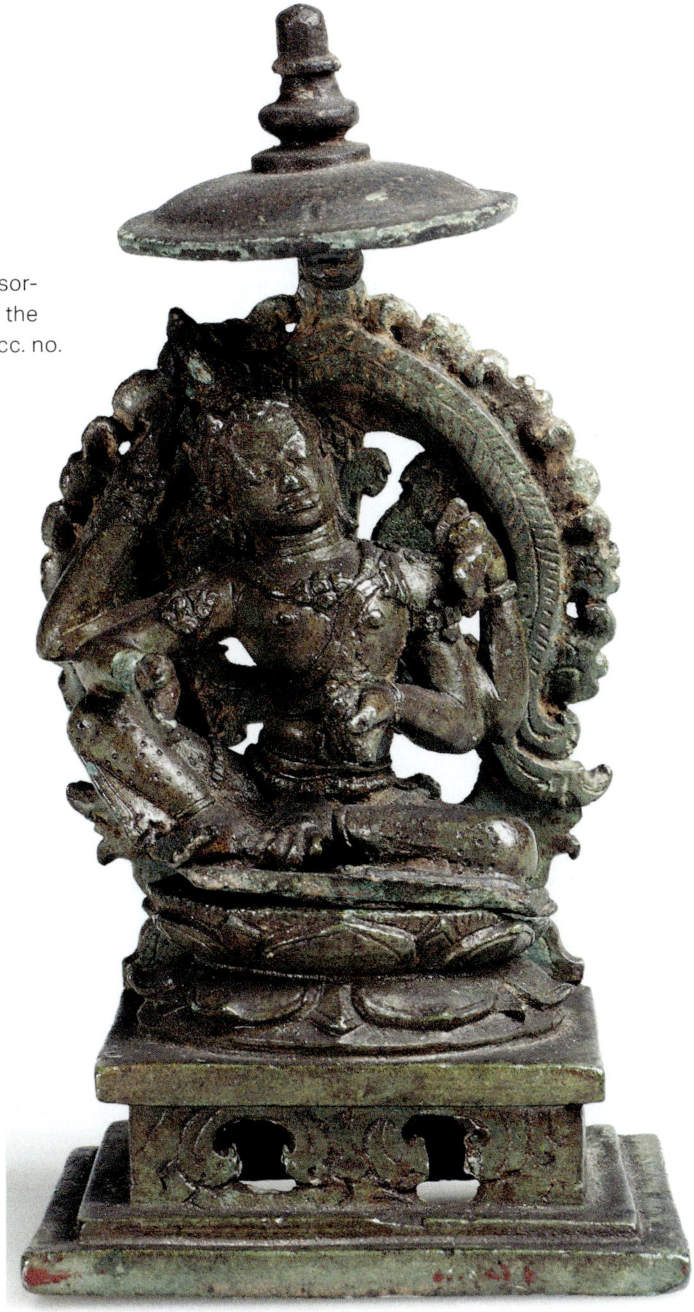

Image 33. Four-armed sorrowful Avalokiteśvara in the Volkenkunde, Leiden. Acc. no. RV-1403-1773.

upper right hand gently touches the leaning head and the lower right hand displays the gift-giving gesture. The upper left hand holds a palm-leaf manuscript and the lower left hand a wish-fulfilling jewel. The presence of the incised holes into the base allows us to date this statuette to between 850-900 CE, the latter part of the Central Javanese period.

Java is exceptional among all the areas in Southeast Asia due to its large production of Avalokiteśvara images. They were primarily produced in bronze, but also in gold, silver and stone. The four-armed sorrowful Avalokiteśvara, where the Bodhisattva's head leans to the right, was an iconographic combination developed in Java. This iconographic form did not spread to other parts of Southeast Asia, illustrating the unique local Javanese artistic language, showing that the Javanese people were interested in images of Avalokiteśvara displaying sorrow. Thus, there were developments in the Buddhism followed on Java, which was separate from the initial cultural influence from South Asia.

The sorrowful Avalokiteśvara symbolises the Bodhisattva's compassion as it shows him feeling sorrow when he sees the suffering in the world. Combined with the use of the wish-fulfilling jewel and a manuscript the images show that Avalokiteśvara is capable of fulfilling all wishes, but also that the Buddhist texts are vital in moving towards enlightenment and the end of all suffering.

7

Thailand – Avalokiteśvaras of Prasat Muang Singh

Thailand has a long and rich history with Buddhism and Buddhist art that remains to this day. Even now, people will visit the Emerald Buddha in Bangkok in order to show their devotion and the many Buddhist temples in Thailand continue to thrive.

Early Buddhist art from this area showed the same type of pan-Southeast Asian cultural response, which was discussed in the first chapter. The artistic language later evolved into two separate styles, one produced in what is now Mainland Thailand and the other in Peninsular Malaya. During this period there were a limited number of Avalokiteśvara images being produced as there was a local focus on Buddha images. However, the Buddhist art from the late twelfth to the early thirteenth century CE shows a strong Khmer influence as parts of modern Thailand were under Khmer rule. The provincial capital of the Khmer empire was located in Lopburi province, north of Bangkok in central Thailand, from the eleventh to the thirteenth century CE. The art created there is often referred to as Lopburi style.

This style is epitomised by several Avalokiteśvara statues that are now on display at the National Museum in Bangkok. Six of these statues were found at a temple site, Prasat Muang Singh

Image 34. Prasat Muang Singh in Kanchanaburi province in western Thailand.

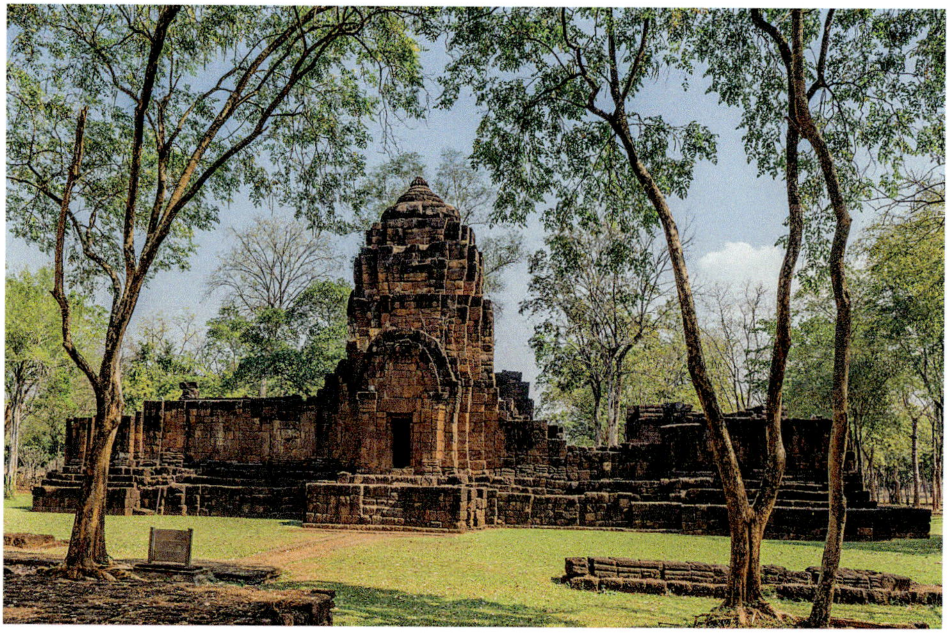

(temple at Muang Singh) in Kanchanaburi province in western Thailand (Image 34).

The temple is found at the centre of Muang Singh, an ancient town on the Kwae Noi river. The town has both earthen ramparts and 5 metre high laterite walls that follow along the river. Laterite is a fantastic building material that is a type of mud that can be cut into bricks and then dried in the sun (Image 35). Laterite is also the main building material of the temple at Muang Singh as well as for side monuments. The quarry for these bricks can be found to the east of Muang Singh.

Image 35. Laterite bricks.

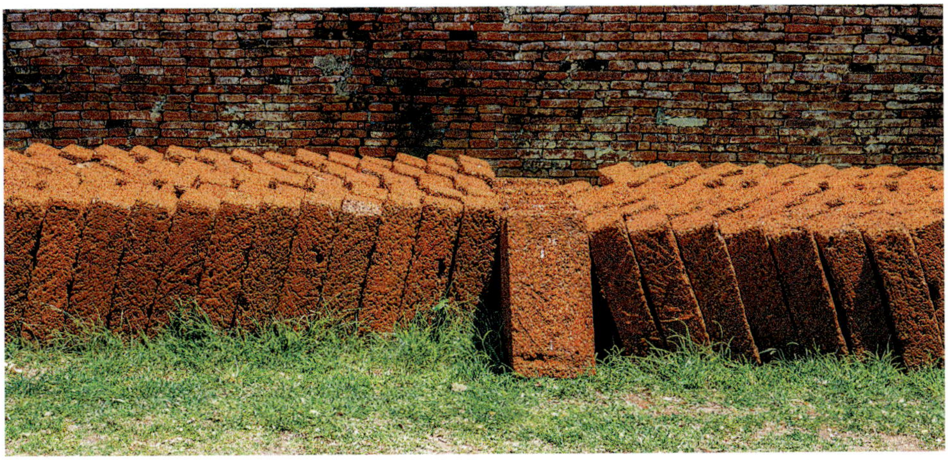

Prasat Muang Singh is the westernmost Khmer temple, making it one of the furthest of the seat of power for the Khmer ruler in Cambodia. The temple has been dated based on the various Buddhist images found at the site. These show a strong influence from the Bayon style of the Khmer ruler Jayavarman VII, which would at least date these images to approximately the late twelfth to the early thirteenth century CE. The temple did not just consist of laterite bricks and sandstone statues. During the restoration there was evidence of stucco decorating the temple and the laterite functioned more as a base on which to decorate. Remnant of the stucco images can be seen at the National Museum in Bangkok.

During the late 1970s, another building construction was found when excavating an earth mound to the north-east of the central temple. The structure was never finished and eventually became covered with earth, finally being excavated by the Fine Arts Department of the Royal Thai Government. It was here that six sandstone statues of Avalokiteśvara were found. They were not found grouped together, but rather in various parts of the building.

As the structure was unfinished there is no firm architectural plan, but the intent of the builders appears to have been to create several small rooms which were connected to each other via corridors. It is in these rooms that the different statues have been found, including a statue of the female Prajñāpāramitā.

These statues depict the standing Avalokiteśvara with four arms. Many of these arms have been damaged due to the ravages of time. However, the upper right hand is still intact in the first of these images (Image 36). In this hand Avalokiteśvara holds a rosary, an attribute we have seen for the Central Javanese statuettes of the sorrowful Avalokiteśvara. This statue was found in the western gallery of the north-western structure, and has a height of 109 cm.

There is also a sculpture where the head is intact, but all of the arms are now missing (Image 37). This statue has a height of 112 cm and was found in the western gallery of the north-western building. The strong similarity between these two statues indicate that they were produced by the same sculptor.

We have even better luck in the third image, where three of the four hands remain intact (Image 38). The lower right hand holds a small lotus bud. The upper left hand holds a book or palm-leaf manuscript and the lower left hand a water vessel.

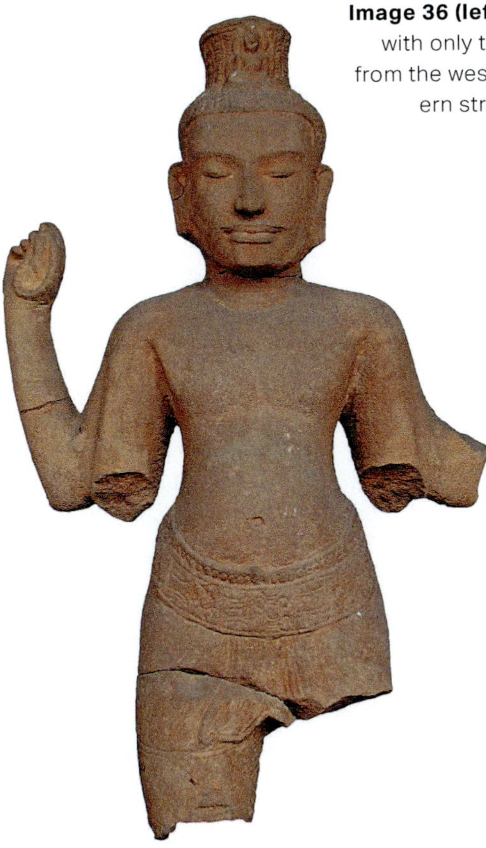

Image 36 (left). Four-armed Avalokiteśvara with only the upper right hand remaining from the western gallery in the north-western structure at Prasat Muang Singh.

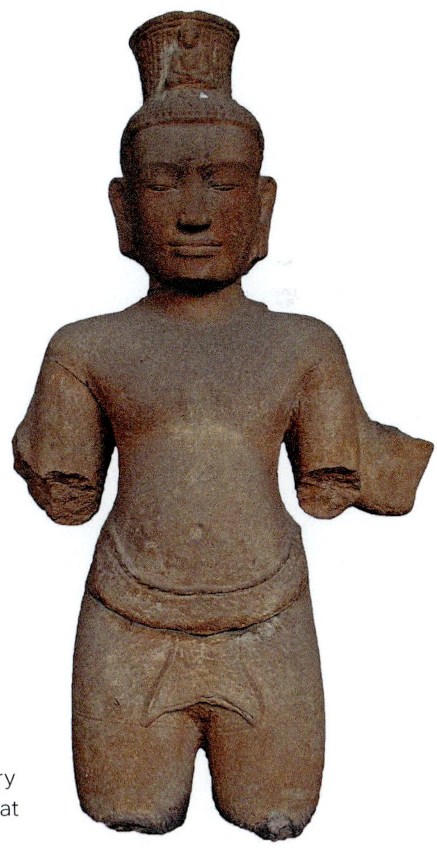

Image 37 (right). Four-armed Avalokiteśvara from the western gallery in the north-western structure at Prasat Muang Singh.

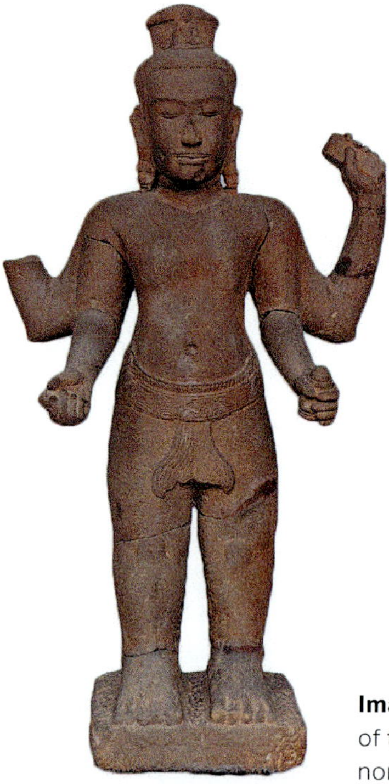

Image 38. Four-armed Avalokiteśvara with three of the hands intact from the northern gallery in the north-western structure at Prasat Muang Singh.

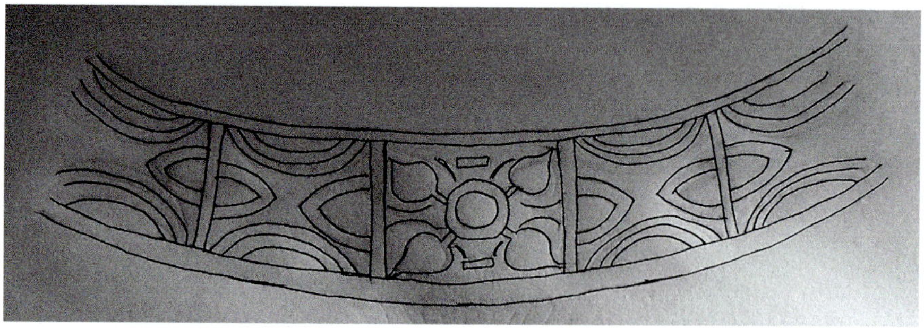

Image 39. Drawing of belt pattern.

This figure also wears earrings, but lacks the common necklace and armbands that we saw for the other Avalokiteśvara images in the previous chapters.

This sandstone sculpture of the four-armed Avalokiteśvara was found in the northern gallery of the north-western monument. It has a height of 161 cm, with the legs and the base intact.

All of these Prasat Muang Singh Avalokiteśvara statues have a particular style of headdress. It has a cylindrical shape with the rounded top that is slightly wider than the cylindrical body. The faces of the Bodhisattvas show closed eyes indicating that the Bodhisattva is in meditation. Each of these statues also have the same mode of dress, a short lower garment where part of the textile is pulled up under the belt creating a fish-tail effect. The belt itself has a beautiful pattern, representing a woven belt embroidered with a floral pattern (Image 39).

There is some difference in the amount of jewellery that these Avalokiteśvaras wear. The two statues from the western gallery in the monument wear no jewellery, but the statue found in the northern gallery has earrings. The western gallery statues also have a different facial shape (round) than the statue from the northern gallery (rectangular). Considering the similarity of the two statues found in the western gallery it is likely that they were made by the same stone cutter. This artist may have worked on site or as these statues exhibit the Lopburi style, they may have been produced at Lopburi and then transported to the temple site at Muang Singh.

The importance of images

None of these Avalokiteśvara statues have survived through the ravages of time without some loss. However, just like the Venus de Milo in the Louvre in Paris, a few missing limbs do

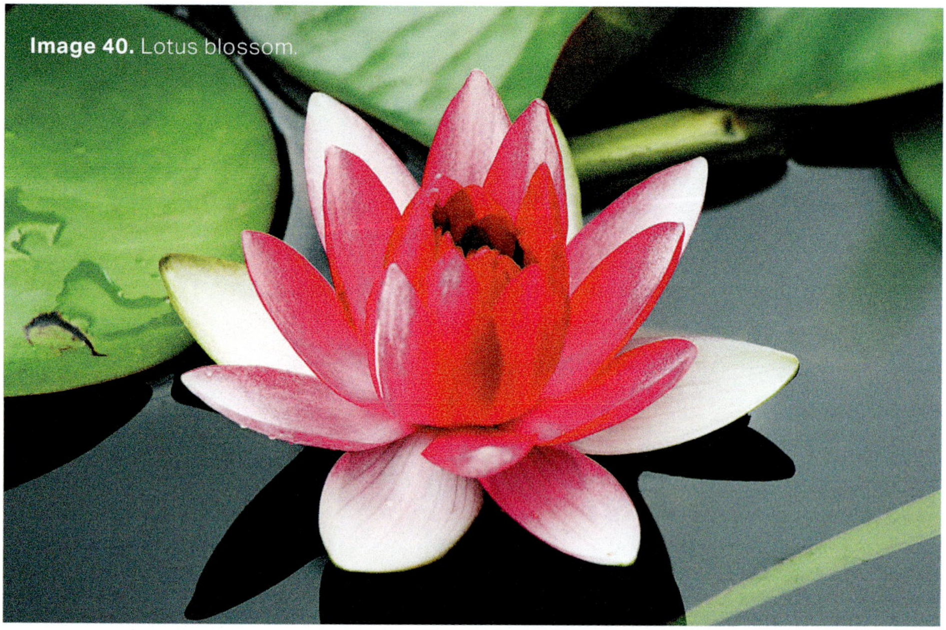

Image 40. Lotus blossom.

not detract from the importance of these sculptures. Venus de Milo's body shape still contains her beauty. With the statues from Prasat Muang Singh, we do not see a sensual body shape, but rather a solidity, a firmness and a directness.

The solid shape gives the viewer a sense of safety and protection. Here Avalokiteśvara is seen as an unmoveable guardian in the storms of life. Add to this the different attributes carried by the Bodhisattva: a lotus, a rosary, a manuscript and a water vessel. Once again, the lotus symbolises purity and strength as it reminds the devotee that it remains untouched by both the water and the mud in which it grows (Image 40).

The presence of the water vessel, a feature of the ascetic Avalokiteśvara, refers back to the earliest Avalokiteśvara images in Southeast Asia as we saw in the Introduction and in Chapter 2 on the Champa bronzes. This shows that these statues are a development of the early images of

Avalokiteśvara in the region, illustrating a continuity of the worship of the Bodhisattva. The manuscript appears in Avalokiteśvara's hands across Southeast Asia and signals his connections with the Buddhist texts, such as the *Lotus Sutra*. In addition, the first statue from Prasat Muang Singh carries a rosary. This attribute is often used by Buddhists to help count the number of times a mantra or prayer is recited. A Buddhist rosary traditionally has 108 beads. A mantra should be recited 100 times, but as we are all fallible a further eight beads are added to the rosary to account for the times we are not focused during the prayers or recitations.

There are no inscriptions from the temple site that explain why these similar statues were all placed in different galleries in the building. Even if these Avalokiteśvara statues had been part of a mandala or a system of images other iconographic forms of the Bodhisattva would have been used. In Buddhist art there are instances where one cave or temple has several depictions of the same figure. At Candi Mendut in Central Java, there are three different forms of Avalokiteśvara. Another example is at Mogao Cave 146, near Dunhuang in China. The cave images date to 776 CE, several centuries before the construction of Prasat Muang Singh. In the cave we see four-armed and eight-armed Avalokiteśvaras, along with Amoghapāśa and the thousand-armed Avalokiteśvara. Thus, there can be several images of Avalokiteśvara in one place, but they normally take different forms, which is what makes the statues from the north-western monument of Prasat Muang Singh unique.

It is possible that the statues were stored in this building before they were to be placed elsewhere, but the temple was then abandoned. However, if that had been the case then the statues would likely have been placed in the same room and not in different rooms in the building. Yet, there is one area of Buddhist imagery where there is a repeated production of the same image – clay tablets. In these cases, the maker has a mould and stamps out repeated images in clay. This type of image production may have influenced the carving of these statues with a similar iconography and style for one building.

The general outline of this north-western monument indicates that it was initially intended as a temple. Considering the number of Avalokiteśvara statues found within the structure, the temple was likely to be dedicated to the Bodhisattva Avalokiteśvara. There is further evidence to support this theory as there is a relief carved into the laterite walls of the structure signifying the Bodhisattva. Unfortunately, laterite does not hold great detail and it is likely the relief was once covered by stucco. Yet, this building is secondary to the main temple at the site, where other images have been found. Among these are Prajñāpāramitā statues, Avalokiteśvara statues, a Buddha and one Radiant Avalokiteśvara which will be discussed further in the next chapter.

8

Cambodia – the Radiant Avalokiteśvara

Modern day Cambodia has a long history with Buddhism, but may be most well-known for Angkor Wat and Angkor Thom. Angkor Wat is a temple city that illustrated the king's divinity, as well as a Hindu pantheon. This site with its tall towers has stood the test of time and after extensive studies and renovations is now under the protection of UNESCO as a World Heritage Site. However, Angkor Wat is far from the only temple or city to have been built near the large lake, the Tonlé Sap, and its flood plains.

Angkor Thom (Holy City), an even greater city than Angkor Wat, was built over time in the shape of a perfect square surrounded by a moat. Research is still ongoing to determine how many people lived in this city. At the centre of the city stands the Bayon temple, famous for its tall towers with the large serene faces that would have looked out over Angkor Thom (Image 41).

Hinduism was the Khmer state religion from the second century onwards, but there were certain rulers and of course other people who followed Buddhism. Perhaps the most famous Buddhist ruler was Jayavarman VII (reigned 1181-1218 CE), who is also known as the Builder King. He

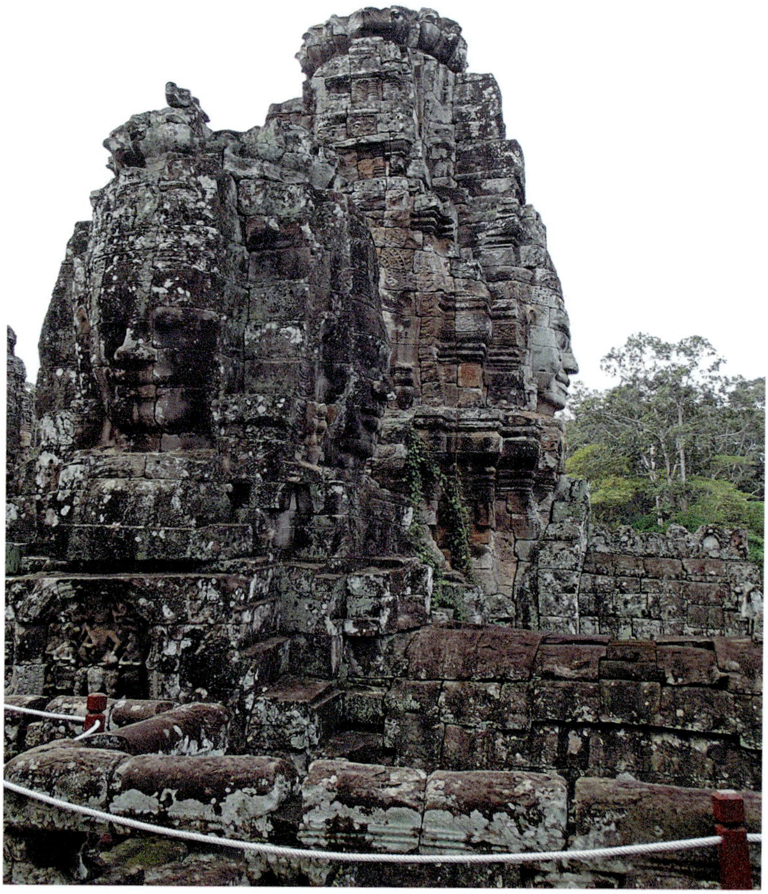

Image 41. The Bayon temple at Angkor Thom in Cambodia.

made great investments into the local infrastructure, such as building roads and rest houses one day's journey apart. He also had many temples constructed. We have already examined one of these temples, the temple at Muang Singh in Thailand, in the previous chapter. Jayavarman VII also had other temples built closer to the capital city, such as Ta Prohm and Preah Khan (Image 42).

Image 42. Preah Khan in Cambodia.

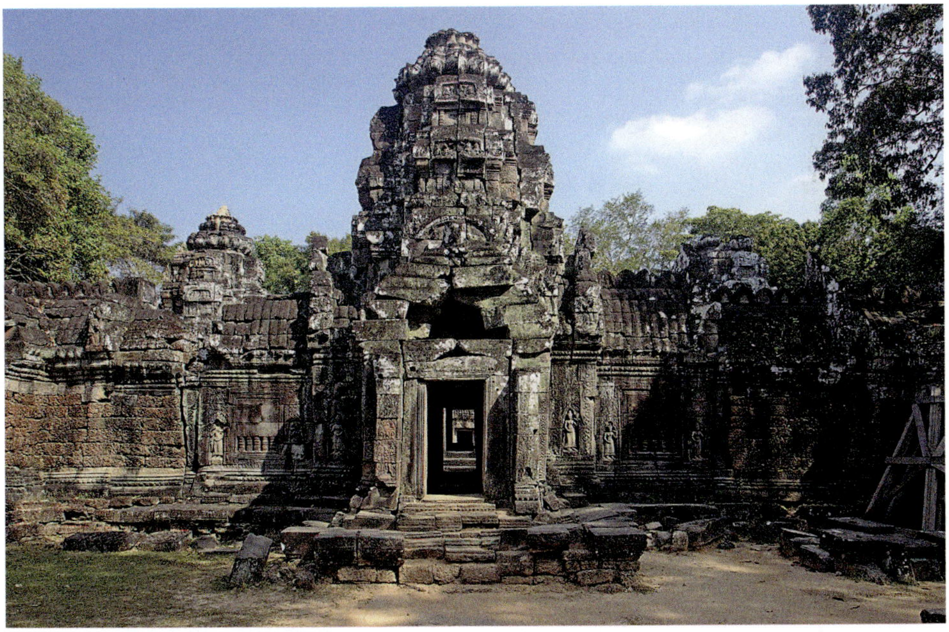

It was during Jayavarman VII's rule that a new iconographic form was developed for Avalokiteśvara, which is today known as the Radiant Avalokiteśvara. It shows the Bodhisattva as standing and with eight arms. Incised into his body are images of Buddhas in meditation as well as female figures. The Radiant Avalokiteśvara statues have been found at different sites in both Cambodia and Thailand, but it is specifically associated with Preah Khan (Image 43).

It was at this temple that an inscription was found, dating to 1191 CE. The inscription invoked the Buddha,

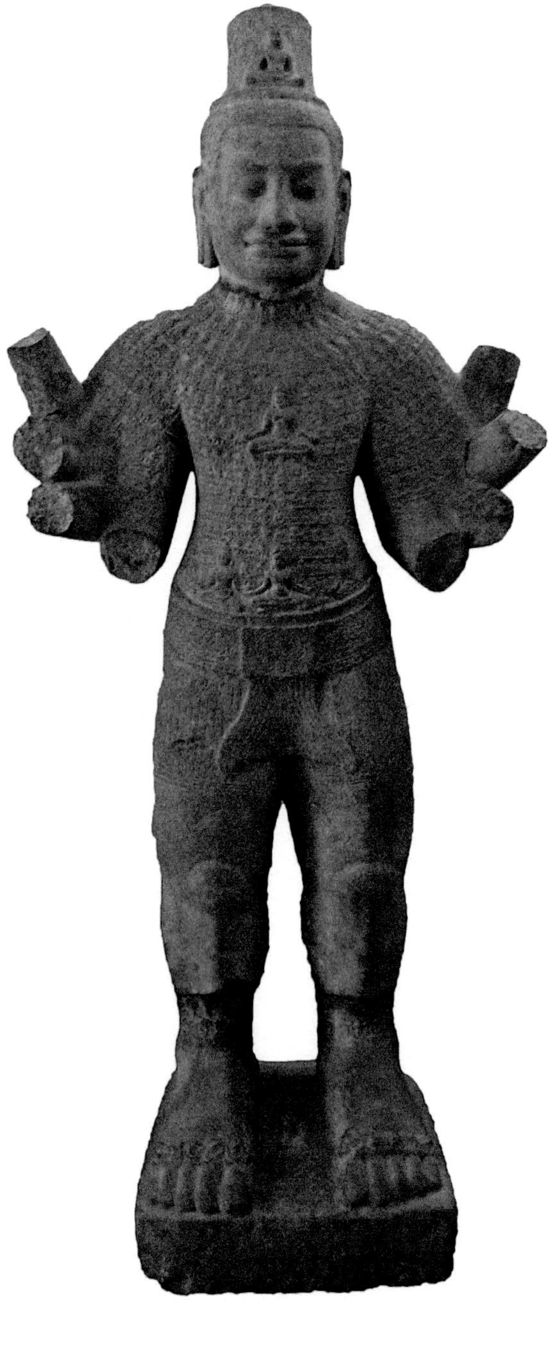

Avalokiteśvara and Prajñāpāramitā (the goddess of wisdom and a representation of the Buddhist text – the *Prajñāpāramitā-sūtra*). The inscription describes Avalokiteśvara as a walking tree, where his arms are branches. He is the source of all that can be desired. The metaphor of a walking wish-fulfilling tree references the separate realms of the Buddhas, such as Sukhāvatī paradise, the home of the Buddha Amitābha who we see in Avalokiteśvara's headdress. In Sukhāvatī paradise there are wish-fulfilling jewels that can grant any desire. We saw Avalokiteśvara hold such a jewel in the chapter on Javanese bronze statuettes. The Preah Khan inscription also mentions a further 23 statues named Jayabuddhamahānātha, that were sent to various places in the

Image 43. Radiant Avalokiteśvara in the National Museum, Bangkok.

Khmer kingdom including Angkor Thom and Phimae. These are the statues that are today known as Radiant Avalokiteśvara.

This stone statue shows Avalokiteśvara as standing and with eight arms (Image 43). Unfortunately, none of the arms have been found intact, therefore we cannot be sure which attributes of gestures the Bodhisattva displayed. The Radiant Avalokiteśvara is unusual as there are other figures carved into the Bodhisattva's body. Seated meditating Buddhas can be seen on Avalokiteśvara's headdress, his torso, arms, ankles and feet. In the centre of Avalokiteśvara's chest sits a female figure with her arms extended to either side. Above the Bodhisattva's belt sits a line of similar female figures, these holding hands with each other.

The seated female figure at the centre of Avalokiteśvara's torso may be a representation of Prajñāpāramitā, the mother of the Buddhas. She is often depicted alongside the Buddha and Avalokiteśvara in Khmer triads. The females seated, holding hands, just above the lower garment can also be found at the Bayon in Angkor Thom. The Bayon towers, with its serene faces, have female figures just below the faces with their arms outstretched so they can reach each other. It is unlikely that they also represent Prajñāpāramitā. They could be females that are a part of a mandala or ritual where they form the border, or they may represent another of Avalokiteśvara's pores.

The presence of the meditating Buddhas references the description of Avalokiteśvara in the Buddhist text, *Kārandavyūhasūtra* (*Casket of the qualities of Avalokiteśvara*). The text tells of Avalokiteśvara's twelve pores, where each is a separate world with 100 Buddhas. In the Radiant Avalokiteśvara, the Bodhisattva's body is the entire universe where each of his pores contains a separate world. We have previously seen him in a more worldly form, where he carries attributes linking his image to Buddhist texts and rituals.

> Sarvanīvaraṇaviṣkambhin, it is like this: A trillion gandharvas (heavenly being) dwell in a pore named Suvarṇa. They do not experience the sufferings of *saṃsāra* and are satisfied by perfect happiness. They perceive divine objects but are free of attachment. They have no aversion, they do not become angry, and they never have malice (*Kāraṇḍavyūhasūtra*: 49).

In the *Kāraṇḍavyūhasūtra*, the Bodhisattva Sarvanīvaraṇaviṣkambhin asks the Buddha if he could visit these wondrous worlds in each of Avalokiteśvara's pores. However, the Buddha tells him of another Bodhisattva, Samantabhadra, who travelled and explored the pores for 12 years, but never saw the Buddhas who reside in each pore. If such a great Bodhisattva could not do it, then what chance would other Bodhisattvas have? Yet, it is the presence of these Buddhas that allows Avalokiteśvara to produce merit.

> Noble son, Bodhisattva Mahāsattva Avalokiteśvara has those samādhis (stillness of mind). In each of his pores there are a hundred thousand samādhis. Noble son, in that way, Bodhisattva Mahāsattva Avalokiteśvara has an

> incalculable accumulation of merit. Even the tathāgatas (Buddhas) do not have this kind of accumulation of merit, let alone a bodhisattva (*Kāraṇḍavyūhasūtra*: 46).

Unfortunately, none of the stone Radiant Avalokiteśvara's hands have survived. However, we find a relief of another type of Avalokiteśvara with multiple arms at the temple Banteay Chhmar (Image 44).

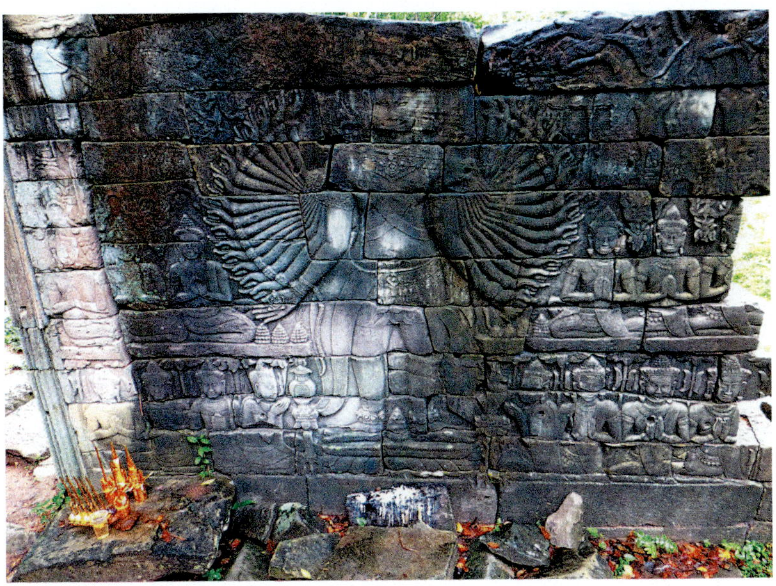

Image 44. Eleven-headed and thousand-armed Avalokiteśvara at Banteay Chhmar, Cambodia.

Image 45. Female apsara in stone from the Bayon, Angkor Thom, Cambodia.

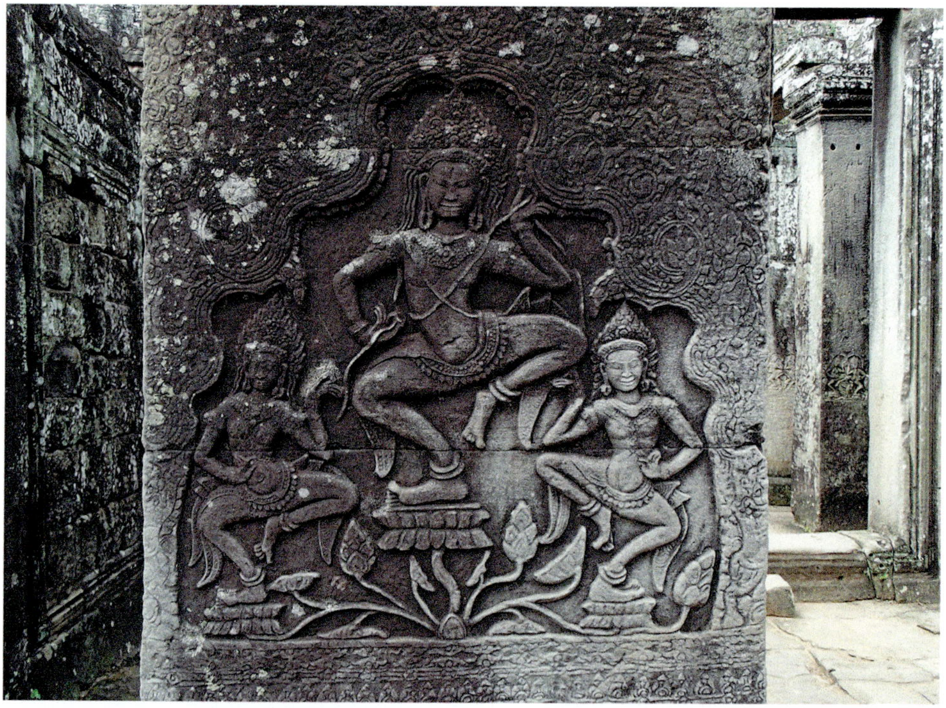

This temple is located close to the Thai-Cambodian border and has suffered a great deal of looting. Once, there were eight large reliefs depicting the Bodhisattva Avalokiteśvara, but now only two remain at the site. Banteay Chhmar was constructed during the reign of Jayavarman VII, who commissioned the Radiant Avalokiteśvaras. The relief is on one of the walls and shows Avalokiteśvara with eleven heads and a thousand arms.

Only the lowest hand on either side shows any attribute. In his lowest right hand, Avalokiteśvara holds a small seated figure with four arms. The figure is too small to be identified, but it is likely another form of Avalokiteśvara as any Buddha usually only has two arms. The figure's two lower hands are joined in the meditation gesture, while the attributes in the two upper hands cannot be determined. The eleven-headed and thousand-armed Avalokiteśvara holds a water vessel in his lower left hand. Based on this information we may speculate that the Radiant Avalokiteśvara once held a water vessel as well as displayed one of Avalokiteśvara's more common gestures, such as the gift-giving gesture.

The seated female figures along the waist of the Radiant Avalokiteśvara likely represent *apsaras*, a type of deity within Buddhist cosmology (Image 45). They are known as beautiful dancers and can often be seen depicted on Khmer temples. They reside in one of Avalokiteśvara's pores named Ratnakuṇḍala, where *ratna* means a jewel or treasure and *kuṇḍala* is a ring.

Jayavarman VII placed the Radiant Avalokiteśvara stone statues in the Buddhist temples throughout his kingdom. This may in part have been a way for the ruler to gain merit, for his people and his country. Yet, there could also have been political implications behind his decision. By ordering the construction of temples and roads that could lead pilgrims to these temples, Jayavarman VII was also expanding the Khmer cultural presence in the region. This even reached as far as Muang Singh in modern western Thailand.

Image 46. Radiant Avalokiteśvara found at Prasat Muang Singh in western Thailand.

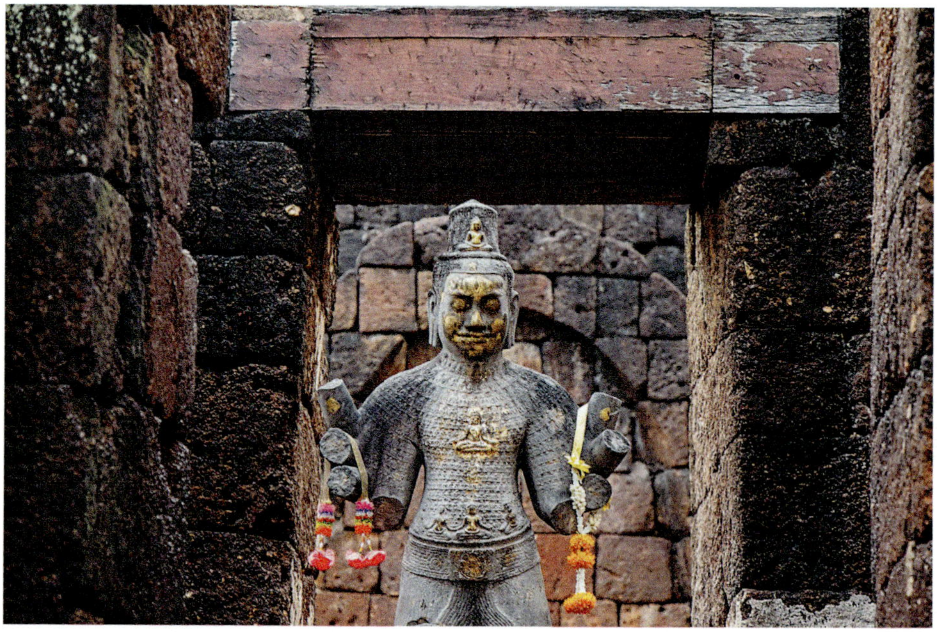

It was in the previous chapter on Prasat Muang Singh in Thailand that we first came across the Radiant Avalokiteśvara. A statue of this iconographic form was found in the central temple building in the Muang Singh temple complex (Image 46).

The Khmer empire was predominantly Hindu, where Angkor Wat was dedicated to Vishnu. Even during the reign of Buddhist rulers there remained elements of Hinduism in state rituals. Utilising the *Kāraṇḍavyūhasūtra* in creating new Buddhist imagery there may have been an attempt to elevate

Buddhism and Avalokiteśvara above Hinduism. For example, the older text, the Lotus Sutra, describes Avalokiteśvara in his more compassionate appearance. He is seen as a rescuer from danger and a teacher of the Buddhist law who can take on any form. However, in the *Kāraṇḍavyūhasūtra* Avalokiteśvara cannot just take on any shape, he also gives birth to Vedic gods such as the sun and the wind. The text even describes Avalokiteśvara as speaking with Shiva, who prostrates himself before the Bodhisattva, placing Avalokiteśvara in a higher level of power.

The description of pores and separate worlds within Avalokiteśvara's body is a metaphor in order that worshippers reading the *Kāraṇḍavyūhasūtra* or seeing the Radiant Avalokiteśvara could understand the greatness that is encompassed by the Bodhisattva Avalokiteśvara. The Radiant Avalokiteśvara was simply a new way of illustrating the compassion and power of the Bodhisattva. With his pores of different worlds, each containing 100 Buddhas, we may better understand how Avalokiteśvara can be an endless source of merit.

9

Conclusion

The Bodhisattva Avalokiteśvara remains a strong presence in today's Buddhist countries of Southeast Asia, such as Singapore, Thailand and Vietnam. However, he also had a great cultural impact on this region 1,000 years ago. As we have seen in the images of Avalokiteśvara in this book, no matter where in Southeast Asia they were found, they all illustrate the Bodhisattva in a calm and peaceful manner (Image 47).

Demonstrating and communicating the Bodhisattva's compassion through images alone is no easy task for a craftsman and the local artists primarily

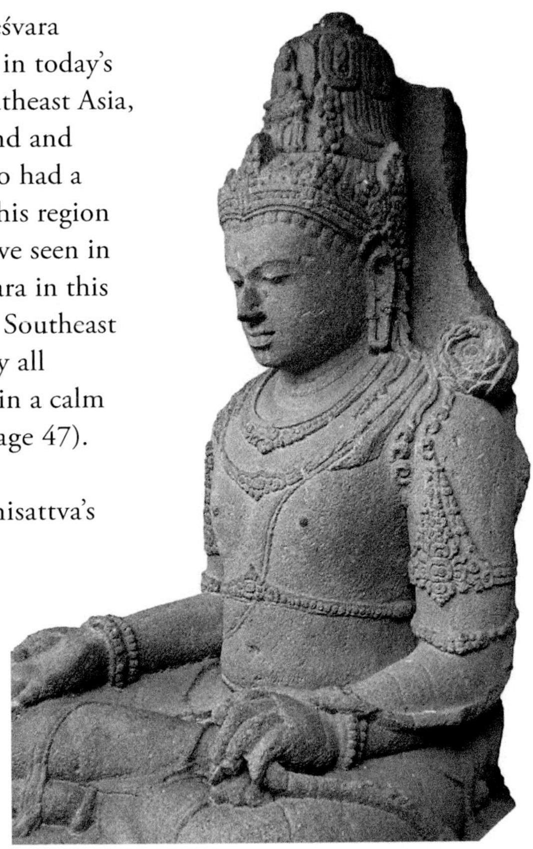

Image 47. Two-armed seated Avalokiteśvara found in Central Java.

used iconographic features to communicate this ideal to the worshippers. The viewer of the Avalokiteśvara image in the Buddhist period in Southeast Asia needed to have a certain knowledge regarding the meaning of the various symbols depicted with the figure. Yet, centuries later a viewer from a completely different era can see the same images and read the same message. A message left by a culture, which has long since evolved with the times.

The bronze and stone workers managed to connect the Avalokiteśvara images to different Buddhist texts through the use of hand gestures and attribute iconography. As we saw in the Introduction there was a general knowledge regarding Avalokiteśvara images spread over Southeast Asia, however, over time the metal workers developed a local style that helps us date these statuettes. The earliest Avalokiteśvara statuettes and statues show him primarily displaying the gift-giving gesture and a lotus. This evolved into figures with four or eight arms that would display the sorrowful gesture or the fearlessness gesture as well.

Yet, Avalokiteśvara images from across Southeast Asia share a common attribute – the lotus. References to lotuses in Buddhist texts use it as a simile in teaching or as a symbol for that purity can come from the mud. In the *Milinda Pañha*, the monk Nagasena answers questions from the Indo-Greek king Menander I about Buddhism.

> The Elder (Nagasena) replied: Is there such a thing, O king, as a lotus flower with hundred petals?
> Yes, there is.
> Where does it grow up?
> It is produced in mud, and in water it comes to perfection.
> But does the lotus resemble the mud of the lake, whence it springs up, either in colour, or in smell, or in taste?
> Certainly not.
> Then does it resemble the water?
> Not that either.
> Just so, great king, is it that the Blessed One had the bodily signs and marks you have mentioned, though his parents had them not.
> Well answered, Nagasena" (Rhys Davids 2001: 117).

Even though we all know what a lotus looks like, each area of Southeast Asia designed their own style of lotus for the Avalokiteśvara images. These localised designs illustrate the development of the local artistic language among the producers of Buddhist imagery 1,000 years ago.

Previous studies in the 1900s of Southeast Asian Buddhist art posited that the local artist simply copied Indian examples or that Southeast Asia even imported images instead of producing their own. This is far from the truth as each area developed its own iconography and style for Buddhist images. Java is an excellent example of a culture that absorbed cultural input from South Asia, but was not a passive partner in the transference. From the earliest Avalokiteśvara images in Java, we see local stylistic features and these developed over time. The Javanese were never a passive partner, but actively adapted Buddhist art to suit their own preferences.

Who were the sponsors of these many Avalokiteśvara images?

We have seen evidence of donation or funding of Buddhist images, in particular in Java, Thailand and Cambodia. However, this does not just occur within the Buddhist faith, we also see this in in Hinduism and Christianity. One of the famous periods of European history was in Florence during the Medici's reign. Their funding of religious imagery led to the production of buildings, paintings and sculptures by artists such as Filippo Brunelleschi and Michelangelo Buonarroti. The funding of large-scale monuments such as Borobudur or the Bayon came from the local rulers and has left a lasting impact on the landscape. Rulers such as Jayavarman VII also funded statues as we saw in the chapter on Cambodia and the Radiant Avalokiteśvara.

However, there is not as much evidence for the ruling classes funding the production of the smaller metal statuettes. Yet, the number and the variety of styles of the Avalokiteśvara statuettes show us that they were made by different craftsmen in different workshops and that these must have been spread out over Java, Cambodia and Thailand specifically. In order to fund this many images, there would have been a variety of people who sought these statuettes. These were likely merchants, monks, pilgrims to different temples and perhaps whole villages who wished to have a statuette in a local sanctuary.

I hope that through this book I have managed to pass on some of my love for these beautiful images and their historical importance in Southeast Asia. They stand as a testament to the talents and hard work of local craftsmen and the desire among the population for images of the compassionate Bodhisattva.

> This is the pious gift of a layperson. What merit be therein, let it belong to her parents and all living beings.

Images and drawings

Image credits

Adobe Stock Photos

Anandajoti Bhikkhu. www.photodharma.net

Author

Dr. Véronique Degroot

Gunawan Kartapranata

Metropolitan Museum of Art, New York, U.S.A.

Rijksmuseum, Amsterdam, the Netherlands

Virtual Collection of Asian Masterpieces

Wikimedia Commons

Nationaal Museum van Wereldculturen, Leiden, the Netherlands

Drawings

Author

Manisha Dayal

Jenni Söderlund

List of images

1. Map of Southeast Asia. Adobe Stock Photo (#198963693).
2. Avalokiteśvara headdress illustrating the presence of the Buddha Amitābha seated in meditation. Statue at the Sonobudoyo Museum, Yogyakarta, Indonesia. Photo by author.
3. Ascetic Avalokiteśvara in the Metropolitan Museum of Art, New York, U.S.A. Acc.no. 1987.218.16
4. Ascetic Avalokiteśvara stone statue with an antelope skin in the Bangkok National Museum. Photograph by Anandajoti Bhikkhu. https://www.photodharma.net/Thailand/National-Museum/National-Museum.htm
5. Four-armed Avalokiteśvara from the Museum Nasional. Photograph by Anandajoti Bhikkhu. https://www.photodharma.net/Indonesia/28-National-Museum/28-National-Museum.htm
6. Example of a two-armed ascetic Avalokiteśvara in bronze from the Metropolitan Museum of Art, New York, U.S.A. Acc. no. 1987.142.223.
7. Example of Champa architecture from the Hindu complex My Son, Vietnam. Adobe Stock Photo (#197769645).
8. Four-armed ascetic Avalokiteśvara the National Museum of Vietnamese History in Ho Chi Minh City. Acc. no. BTLS 1290. Photo by Daderoton commons.wikimedia.org.
9. Four-armed bejeweled Avalokiteśvara in the National Museum of Vietnamese History in Ho Chi Minh City. Acc. no. BTLS 1289. Photo by Daderot commons.wikimedia.org.
10. Example of a bronze with a more realistic style of dress from Peninsular Malaya. Drawing by Manisha Dayal.

11. Eight-armed Amoghapāśa Lokeśvara from Perak in Malaysia. Image courtesy of Virtual Collection of Asian Masterpieces. Acc. No. MN.BALAIB.40.2008.
12. Gesture of fearlessness, the *abhaya-mudrā*. Photo by author.
13. Eight-armed seated Amoghapāśa Lokeśvara in the Museum Nasional, Jakarta, Indonesia. Photo by author. Acc. no. 603.
14. Amoghapāśa Lokeśvara plaque in the Metropolitan Museum of Art, New York, U.S.A. Acc. no. 2014.517.
15. Back of the Amoghapāśa Lokeśvara plaque in the Metropolitan Museum of Art, New York, U.S.A. Acc. no. 2014.517.
16. Four-armed bejeweled golden Avalokiteśvara from Sumatra, Indonesia. Photo by Dr. V. Degroot.
17. Four-armed Avalokiteśvara with a hollow niche in the headdress, Sumatra, Indonesia. Photo by Dr. V. Degroot.
18. The gift-giving gesture or *varada-mudrā* gesture. Drawing by Manisha Dayal.
19. Golden four-armed Avalokiteśvara with a circular halo in the British Museum, London, U.K. Acc. no. 1956,0725.4. Drawing by Jenni Söderlund.
20. Two-armed Avalokiteśvara from the Sambas hoard in the British Museum, London, U.K. Acc. no. 1956,0725.6. Drawing by Manisha Dayal.
21. Four-armed Avalokiteśvara with indented star pattern in the British Museum, London, U.K. Acc. no. 1956,0725.5. Drawing by Jenni Söderlund.
22. Four-armed Avalokiteśvara with no backpiece in the British Museum, London, U.K. Acc. no. 1956,0725.9. Drawing by Manisha Dayal.

23. Four-armed Avalokiteśvara found at Borobudur and now at the Collection Nationaal Museum van Wereldculturen, Leiden, the Netherlands. Coll. no. RV-1403-1841.
24. Relief from the fourth level of Borobudur illustrating the *Bhadracarī*. Photo by author.
25. Two-armed Maitreya from the Prakhon Chai hoard in the Metropolitan Museum of Art, New York, U.S.A. Acc. no. 1994.51.
26. Top level of Borobudur, Java, Indonesia. Adobe Stock Photo (#23367729). Photo by Olga Khoroshunova.
27. Outside image of Candi Mendut, Java, Indonesia. Adobe Stock Photo (# 205820059).
28. Avalokiteśvara inside Candi Mendut, Java, Indonesia. Photo by author.
29. Silhouette of makara at Borobudur, Java, Indonesia. Photo by author.
30. Close up of makara at Prambanan, Java, Indonesia. Photo by author.
31. Four-armed sorrowful Avalokiteśvara in the Museum Nasional, Jakarta, Indonesia. Acc. no. c.134. Photo by author.
32. Four-armed sorrowful Avalokiteśvara in the Rijksmuseum, Amsterdam, the Netherlands. Acc. no. MAK 312.
33. Four-armed sorrowful Avalokiteśvara in the Collection Nationaal Museum van Wereldculturen. Coll. no. RV-1403-1773.
34. Prasat Muang Singh, Thailand. Adobe Stock Photo (#100663411).
35. Laterite bricks. Adobe Stock Photo (#140218671).

36. Four-armed Avalokiteśvara with only the upper right hand remaining from the western gallery in the north-western structure at Prasat Muang Singh. Statue is now at the National Museum, Bangkok, Thailand. Photo by author.
37. Four-armed Avalokiteśvara from the western gallery in the north-western structure at Prasat Muang Singh. Statue is now at the National Museum, Bangkok, Thailand. Photo by author.
38. Four-armed Avalokiteśvara with three of the hands intact from the northern gallery in the north-western structure at Prasat Muang Singh. Statue is now at the National Museum, Bangkok, Thailand. Photo by author.
39. Drawing of belt pattern by author.
40. Lotus blossom. Adobe Stock Photo (#44963121).
41. Bayon at Angkor Thom, Cambodia. Photo by author.
42. Preah Khan, Cambodia. Adobe Stock Photo (#65246767).
43. Radiant Avalokiteśvara in the National Museum, Bangkok, Thailand. Photo by author.
44. Eleven-headed and thousand-armed Avalokiteśvara at Banteay Chhmar. Photo by Anandajoti Bhikkhu (www.photodharma.net/Cambodia/13-Banteay-Chhmar/13-Banteay-Chhmar.htm).
45. Female apsara in stone from the Bayon, Cambodia. Photo by author.
46. Radiant Avalokiteśvara found at Prasat Muang Singh in western Thailand. Adobe Stock Photo (#124042392).
47. Two-armed seated Avalokiteśvara found in Central Java at the Sonobudoyo Museum, Yogyakarta, Java, Indonesia. Photo by author.

References and recommended reading

Bhattacharyya, B. 1958. *The Indian Buddhist iconography: mainly based on the Sādhanamālā and cognate Tāntric texts of rituals.* Calcutta: Mukhopadhyay.

Boisselier, J. 1957. "A propos d'un bronze cham inédit d'Avalokiteçvara." *Arts Asiatiques* 4: 255-274.

Chutiwongs, N. 2002. *The iconography of Avalokiteśvara in Mainland South East Asia.* New Delhi: Aryan.

Conze, E. and I.B. Horner, D. Snellgrove, A. Waley. 2014. *Buddhist texts through the ages.* London: Oneworld Publications.

Gosling, B. 2004. *Origins of Thai art.* Bangkok: River Books.

Kāraṇḍavyūha. The Basket's Display. Translated by P.A. Roberts with T. Yeshi. 84000.co.

Kern, J.H.C. 1884. *The Saddharma-Pundarîka or, The lotus of the True Law*. Oxford: The Clarendon Press.

Krairiksh, P. 2012. *The roots of Thai art.* Bangkok: River Books.

Lunsingh Scheurleer, P. and M.J. Klokke. 1988. *Divine bronze: ancient Indonesian bronzes from A.D. 600 to 1600.* Leiden: Brill.

Manguin, P-Y. 2011. "Pan-regional responses to South Asian inputs in early Southeast Asia." *50 years of archaeology in Southeast Asia: Essays in honour of Ian Glover*, edited by B. Bellina, E.A. Bacus, T.O. Pryce and J. Wisseman Christie. Bangkok: River Books. Pgs 171-180.

McArthur, M. 2002. *Reading Buddhist art.* London: Thames and Hudson.

Osto, D.E. 2010. "A new translation of the Sanskrit *Bhadracarī* with introduction and notes." *New Zealand Journal of Asian Studies* 12(2): 1-21.

Revire, N. 2016. *The enthroned Buddha in majesty: an iconological study.* Religions. Université Sorbonne Paris Cité.

Rhys Davids, T.W. 2001. *The questions of King Milinda. Vol. 1.* London: RoutledgeCurzon.

Subhadradis Diskul, M.C. 1981. "Further notes on Prasat Muang Singh, Kanchanaburi Province." *Journal of the Siam Society* 69(01): 164-168.

Sundstrom, S. 2013. "Symbolic gestures (*mudrās*)." *Danced Creation. Asia's mythical past and living present*, edited by J. Kuhnt-Saptodevo and B. Zorn. Welt Museum Wien: Brandstätter. Pgs 42-47.

Sundstrom, S. 2015. "The Bodhisattva Avalokiteśvara in the Thai-Malay Peninsula and Western Indonesia: the early development of Buddhist imagery in Insular Southeast Asia." *Rian Thai* 8: 227-256.